THE LONDON
FELTHAM TRAM

THE LONDON
FELTHAM TRAM

THE EVOLUTION OF A CLASSIC TRAMCAR DESIGN

PETER WALLER

PEN & SWORD
TRANSPORT
AN IMPRINT OF PEN & SWORD BOOKS LTD.
YORKSHIRE – PHILADELPHIA

First published in Great Britain in 2020 by
Pen and Sword Transport
An imprint of
Pen & Sword Books Ltd
Yorkshire - Philadelphia

Copyright © Peter Waller, 2020

ISBN 978 1 52670 213 5

The right of Peter Waller to be identified as Author of this work has been asserted by him in accordance with the Copyright, Designs and Patents Act 1988.

A CIP catalogue record for this book is available from the British Library.

All rights reserved. No part of this book may be reproduced or transmitted in any form or by any means, electronic or mechanical including photocopying, recording or by any information storage and retrieval system, without permission from the Publisher in writing.

Typeset in Palatino 11/13 by Aura Technology and Software Services, India.

Printed and bound in India by Replika Press Pvt. Ltd.

Pen & Sword Books Ltd incorporates the Imprints of Pen & Sword Books Archaeology, Atlas, Aviation, Battleground, Discovery, Family History, History, Maritime, Military, Naval, Politics, Railways, Select, Transport, True Crime, Fiction, Frontline Books, Leo Cooper, Praetorian Press, Seaforth Publishing, Wharncliffe and White Owl.

For a complete list of Pen & Sword titles please contact

PEN & SWORD BOOKS LIMITED
47 Church Street, Barnsley, South Yorkshire, S70 2AS, England
E-mail: enquiries@pen-and-sword.co.uk
Website: www.pen-and-sword.co.uk

or

PEN AND SWORD BOOKS
1950 Lawrence Rd, Havertown, PA 19083, USA
E-mail: Uspen-and-sword@casematepublishers.com
Website: www.penandswordbooks.com

CONTENTS

Abbreviations 6
Introduction 7

The Union Construction & Finance Co 8
The Experimental Cars 9
Construction and Development 29
Early Years of Service 34
Last Years in London 54
Sunderland 91
Operation in Leeds 95
Preservation 139

Appendix 143
Bibliography 147

ABBREVIATIONS

BET	British Electric Traction
BTH	British Thomson-Houston
EMB	Electro-Mechanical Brake Co Ltd, West Bromwich
GEC	General Electric Co
LCC	London County Council
LGOC	London General Omnibus Co
LPTB	London Passenger Transport Board
LST	London & Suburban Traction Co
LTE	London Transport Executive
LUT	London United Tramways
MET	Metropolitan Electric Tramways
MV	Metropolitan-Vickers
PAYE	Pay as you enter
South Met	South Metropolitan Tramways & Lighting Co
UCC	Union Construction & Finance Co
UDC	Urban District Council
UERL	Underground Electric Railways Co of London Ltd

INTRODUCTION

This is the first of a series of books that will examine some of the most influential tram designs to have operated in the British Isles. The 'Felthams' were the result of much development work by the MET and the LUT during the 1920s but, by the time of their delivery, the production cars were too late to save the tramways of north London.

Although the 'Felthams' entered service prior to the creation of the LPTB, it was the decision of the newly-created organisation to scrap the vast London tram network by 1941 that meant that these fine tramcars were virtually 'condemned' within a couple of years of entering service. Being relatively new, they were to be transferred away from their traditional haunts to survive through to final conversion of the south London routes during 1950 and 1951. Given a second life, the majority were to see further service in the West Riding of Yorkshire but a reversal of policy led to their final withdrawal in November 1959. The majority of the illustrations in this book have been drawn from the collection of the Online Transport Archive, a UK-registered charity set up to accommodate collections put together by transport enthusiasts who wished to see their precious images secured for the long-term. Photographs from the collections of the late Fred Andrews, the late Geoffrey Ashwell, the late C. Carter, the late Les Collings, Barry Cross, the late F.N.T. Lloyd-Jones, the late Harry Luff, the late D.W.K. Jones, the late R.W.A. Jones, the late J. Joyce, John Meredith, the late Phil Tatt, the late Julian Thompson, the late R.L. Wilson, Ian Wright and the late W.J. Wyse are all represented in this volume. Further information about the archive can be found at: www.onlinetransportarchive.org or email secretary@onlinetransportarchive.org. Other images have been sourced from the collections held by the National Tramway Museum (the late W.A. Camwell, the late Roy Brook, the late Rob Parr and the late Maurice O'Connor). Every effort has been made to ensure correct attribution but, in the event of any errors, please notify the author via the publishers. As usual, I'm grateful to Martin Jenkins for reading through the text and making comment on it. Any errors are the responsibility of the author and again these can be passed to him via the publisher.

THE UNION CONSTRUCTION & FINANCE CO

The company had been established as the Union Construction Co (its name was changed in 1929) by Charles Tyson Yerkes on 16 October 1901 but was to remain dormant until after the First World War. Yerkes was an American financier and business man; born in Pennsylvania in 1837. He had first got involved in public transport in the late 1880s in Chicago but, in August 1900, he became important in the development of the London Underground, establishing the Underground Electric Railways Co of London in 1902. He was to die three years later but his influence was to outlive him by many decades.

The UERL was established to take over and construct three proposed new deep-level underground lines – the Baker Street & Waterloo (later the Bakerloo), the Charing Cross, Euston & Hampstead (later the Northern) and the Great Northern, Piccadilly & Brompton (later the Piccadilly) – which were all opened towards the end of the decade; these companies were merged to form a single company – the London Electric Railway Co – following an Act of Parliament that received the Royal Assent on 26 July 1910. The District, electrified between 1900 and 1905, was also a subsidiary of the UERL. The company's power station at Lots Road supplied electricity to all of the railway lines controlled by the company. The company's interests expanded in 1912 through the acquisition of the London General Omnibus Co and, on 1 January 1913, by the take over of the Central London and City & South London railways.

Both LUT and MET became effective subsidiaries of Underground Electric Railways Co of London on 1 January 1913 when they were taken over by the London & Suburban Traction Co, a joint venture controlled by UERL and BET. The latter company had owned MET since 1901. The LST acquired South Met later in 1913.

The dormant Union Construction Co was activated in the mid-1920s initially to undertake renovation work on rolling stock used on the Central London Railway. Based at Feltham – hence the nickname acquired by the trams supplied to the LUT and MET – the manufacturer was one of those employed in the construction of London Underground Standard Stock with 182 cars being ordered in 1927 for replacement of older stock on the Piccadilly and Bakerloo lines; known as the 1927 Feltham Stock, these cars entered service during 1929 and 1930. A further 53 cars – again for the Piccadilly – were ordered in 1929 and, in 1930, a further train, comprising two power motor cars and four trailers, was ordered. When completed, these were to prove the last items of equipment to be constructed at the Feltham site.

In addition to its work on the 'Feltham' tram, the company was also to be involved in work on the earliest trolleybuses to operate in London. It was to provide the bodies, fitted to AEC-built chasses, for the first sixty trolleybuses acquired by LUT. These were the first trolleybuses in Britain to be fitted with half-cab bodies with fake bonnets (hence the nickname 'Diddler' for the type).

THE EXPERIMENTAL CARS

In late 1919, four senior members of the MET's management – including C.J. Spencer, the tramways manager – went on a fact-finding mission to North America. The group visited a number of US tramways, including New York and Philadelphia, before producing a number of reports for internal use. Spencer looked at tramcar operation and was particularly enthused by the use of trailer cars, the development of passenger-flow and pay as you enter. He also noted that British tramcar manufacturers seemed to be innately conservative in their designs and unwilling to embrace modern technology and production methods.

Following accident damage, 'E' type No 132 – one of a batch of twenty supplied by Brush to the MET in 1905 on Brush Radial trucks – was rebuilt into a test one-man operated tram. The car is seen here in Wood Green depot whilst being rebuilt. Due to the gradients on the loss-making route to Alexandra Palace, on which the rebuilt car was designed to operate, the Ministry of Transport refused to sanction its use. It was subsequently sold to the LUT. (Barry Cross Collection/Online Transport Archive)

Following its purchase by the LUT, No 132 became No 341 and is seen here at Richmond Park Gates in 1923. (Barry Cross Collection/Online Transport Archive)

In addition to No 341, LUT also converted three other trams – Nos 342-44 – to one-man operation. They were used primarily on the Boston Road route and were withdrawn in 1928 when the route reverted to double-deck operation. (Barry Cross Collection/Online Transport Archive)

The MET's next experiment was to develop and patent revolving staircases in order to attempt the operation of better passenger flow. Only one tram – No 315 – was so equipped and this view records one of the platforms with the staircase fitted. The use of the modified stairs resulted in a reduced upper deck capacity. Never popular, the experimental equipment was soon removed. (Barry Cross Collection/Online Transport Archive)

The immediate result of his work was the conversion of a single-deck car – No 132 which had been damaged in an accident on Monday, 5 April 1920 – into a one-man operated car for use on the loss-making route to Alexandra Palace. The rebuilt car entered service in 1921 but, due to the Ministry of Transport's unwillingness to see its use as a one-man car on the steeply graded route, it was sold to LUT – where it became No 341 – the next year. A further three LUT trams – Nos 342-44 – were also converted to one-man operation. The four cars were withdrawn in 1928, when the Boston Road route (over which they operated) was returned to double-deck operation, and scrapped three years later.

The next MET experiment was with passenger flow. Designed and patented in 1923, the design featured revolving staircases to ensure adequate passenger flow through the front exit whilst still permitting the driver access to the controls. One car – 'H' class No 315 of 1912 – was modified to the new design and entered service in late 1923, although experience resulted in further modification. Used primarily between Cricklewood and Barnet, the tram proved unpopular with both passengers and crews and the tram was soon operated with its revolving staircases fixed into their traditional position and with the usual policy of using the rear platform for entry and exit. It was subsequently restored to fixed staircases albeit retaining its slightly lengthened platforms.

In December 1925, Spencer reported that plans had been prepared for a new tram and that, once the design was approved, a model would be produced before the actual tram was constructed at Hendon. The resulting car was No 318, which was completed in early 1927 and nicknamed 'Bluebell' as a result of its non-standard blue livery. The new vehicle cost £3,520 and, due to its construction, weighed some twelve tons – a reduction of some 25 per cent on the weight of the earlier 'H' class bogie cars. The weight reduction was achieved through the use of aluminium panelling for much of the exterior as well

MET No 318 pictured when new in 1927. At the time of the tram's construction, the rules forbade glazing in front of the driver. No 318 was provided with separate cabs for the driver. The side windows were fitted with a clear plastic, which tended to discolour in sunlight, but the front was left unglazed. The cabs themselves were also cramped and attracted criticism from the unions. (Barry Cross Collection/Online Transport Archive)

A side view of No 318 when new showing the rear entrance and front exit. With enclosed platforms, internal bulkheads were dispensed with and the lower-deck floor was level throughout the passenger compartment. The rear folding doors were controlled by the conductor whilst the front were managed by the driver. (Barry Cross Collection/Online Transport Archive)

The lower deck of MET No 318. Seating was provided for twenty-seven on grey green moquette seats. (London Transport/D.W.K. Jones Collection/Online Transport Archive)

THE EXPERIMENTAL CARS • 13

On 17 June 1927, No 318 was involved in a fatal accident when its air brakes failed while descending Barnet Hill. As a result of the accident, the Metropolitan Police notified the company that trams fitted with air brakes only were no longer deemed suitable for operation in London. When rebuilt, No 318 was fitted with both rheostatic and magnetic track braking whilst retaining its air brakes. (D.W.K. Jones Collection/Online Transport Archive)

as other weight-saving measures. The maximum traction bogies, manufactured by Brush, were standard Class 4 units but fitted with 28in wheels to permit the lower floor level. It was fitted with MV101 50hp motors and BTH C597 controllers.

The vehicle was 36ft 4in in length and 7ft 0in in width; passenger accommodation on the upper deck was forty-four – with 2x2 seating – whilst that on the lower was twenty-seven – the majority on 2x1 seats; the seats on the lower deck were covered in grey-green moquette whilst those on the upper were finished in green leatherette. Unveiled to the press on 3 March 1927, No 318 entered service on route 40 – from Cricklewood to Whetstone – nine days later. However, on 17 June 1927, No 318 was involved in a fatal accident when descending Barnet Hill; following a brake failure, the tram collided with the rear of a lorry, killing the tram's driver, Maurice Kent. Presciently, there had been concerns expressed earlier that the lightweight construction might prove inadequate in the event of such an accident. One consequence of the accident was that the Metropolitan Police determined that operation of trams solely with air brakes was no longer permissible.

Following the accident, No 318 returned to Hendon Works for repair. Whilst this was completed, the tram was modified. Replacement B49 controllers were installed as was additional braking equipment. The staircases were slightly amended as were the entrance and exit doors. As modified the tram re-entered service again on route 40 – albeit no longer operating as it had done occasionally beyond Whetstone to

14 • THE LONDON FELTHAM TRAM

Pictured at North Finchley depot in modified form, No 318 shows some of the modifications undertaken following the accident of June 1927; one of the changes was the widening of the entrance doors on the rear platform. The original plywood roof was replaced in 1929 by a more domed structure – as illustrated here – and the panel on the dash stating 'FRONT EXIT CAR' was added in 1931. (Barry Cross Collection/Online Transport Archive)

Ex-MET No 318 is seen in its final guise as LPTB No 2255 in London Transport red and cream, a livery that replaced its earlier blue scheme. By this date the tram also had a much-reduced destination display and fully-glazed windscreen. In addition, the use of the front exit had been abandoned. (D.W.K. Jones Collection/Online Transport Archive)

Barnet – still in its blue livery; this was to change in late 1931 when the car emerged in the standard MET livery. No 318 passed to the LPTB in July 1933 and was renumbered 2255. Under new ownership, No 2255 was to lose its MET livery, being repainted in standard London Transport red and cream. However, it was not to last long in its new ownership; with the gradual conversion of the routes north of the river to trolleybus operation and being non-standard, No 2255 was to be withdrawn in August 1936 and scrapped later the same year at Charlton.

The second of the experimental cars was constructed by the LGOC at Chiswick Works; Lord Ashfield, chairman of the Underground group, had wanted to compare various designs and the LGOC had recently developed the 'NS' type double-deck bus and standard parts used in the construction of this model were to be used in the development of No 319 *Poppy*.

No 319 – which was initially unveiled as No 139 due to a mistake by the paintshop at Chiswick – was fitted with the same style of Brush-built maximum-traction bogies as fitted on No 318. These were again provided with 28in wheels to permit a level floor through the passenger compartment and platforms. The design of the body owed much to the 'NS' type and, again following contemporary regulations, the separate cabs provided for the drivers were

MET No 319 as completed by the LGOC in 1927; when first unveiled the tram was erroneously numbered 139. (Barry Cross Collection/Online Transport Archive)

16 • THE LONDON FELTHAM TRAM

A view towards the platform on the lower deck of No 319; the lower deck could accommodate twenty-eight passengers whilst the upper had seating for thirty-six. The seating on both decks was finished in grey-green moquette. (Barry Cross Collection/Online Transport Archive)

left open. The 50hp motors were supplied by BTH (of the 509AS type) with BTH controllers. The tram was painted in the darker – London General – red than that used on the MET.

Following completion, No 319 was manoeuvred from Chiswick Works onto the LUT track on Chiswick High Road – a somewhat tricky procedure – before it could operate under its own power. Unfortunately, incorrect wiring – soon rectified – delayed its departure and the tram headed to Hounslow depot. It then transferred via Hendon Works to Finchley from where it was introduced to service on route 40 during April 1927. An intermittent fault – not resolved until the car was transferred to Wood Green depot – meant that it failed in service on a number of occasions. Once this problem was resolved, the tram operated on a number of routes based on Wood Green depot.

As a result of the accident in June 1927 that affected No 318, No 319 was temporarily withdrawn pending modification and it re-entered service in November with additional braking; however, on 16 November 1927, No 319 was sold to LUT – for £1,715 – and was renumbered 350 by its new owner. Two years later, it lost its original trucks – required for use in the construction of experimental 'Feltham' No 330 – and received replacement trucks manufactured at Hendon Works. No 350 was to become LPTB No 2317 in July 1933 but was only to survive for a further two years before withdrawal.

In April 1928, Lord Ashfield gave instructions for designs to be prepared for the construction of two experimental tramcars to be built at Feltham. The design work was undertaken by a team led by William Sebastian Graff-Baker; born in Baltimore, in the USA, Graff-Baker had first joined the Metropolitan District Railway in 1909 and rose to become assistant mechanical engineer of the Underground

Now in LUT ownership, No 350 *Poppy* is seen heading westwards with a service on route 57 towards Hounslow. (Barry Cross Collection/Online Transport Archive)

Pictured in 1932, No 350 stands at the stub terminus at Kew Bridge; this was a short working on the longer route 57. Note that by this date No 350 had acquired a san serif fleet number. (Maurice O'Connor/National Tramway Museum)

18 • THE LONDON FELTHAM TRAM

group in 1922, a position that he held until after the creation of the LPTB. In 1935 he became the LPTB's chief mechanical engineer (railways). One of his particular areas of interest was bogie design and he presented a paper to the Institution of Mechanical Engineers on the subject in 1952 shortly before his death. The budget for the two trams was, in theory, £5,000, but this was to be doubled as a result of the modifications undertaken to No 330 during its construction.

MET No 320 recorded when new. Note the small window located in the roof of the driver's cab; this was provided to assist the driver when turning the destination indicator. (Jack Law Collection/Online Transport Archive)

The two prototype 'Felthams' are pictured outside Finchley depot. At 7ft 3¼in in width, No 320 was the widest tram operated by the MET. (London Transport/Barry Cross Collection/Online Transport Archive)

The original plough-fitted trucks fitted to No 320 – one of which is seen here – were built by UCC but proved unsatisfactory in operation with the result that they were quickly replaced by a second set of equal-wheel bogies. Constructed in cast steel and heavier than the originals, the replacement bogies were not plough-fitted. (London Transport/D.W.K. Jones Collection/Online Transport Archive)

When completed, the upper deck of No 320 offered seating for forty passengers; of these, twenty-two were accommodated in three different types of seat – as illustrated here: double bench; double semi-bucket; and single swivelling pedestals. (London Transport/D.W.K. Jones Collection/Online Transport Archive)

The order for the two trams was placed in mid-1928 and the first of the duo – MET No 320 – was completed early the following year. When it emerged in April 1929, No 320 was revolutionary in design. Unlike earlier double-deck trams, which had generally been constructed with lower and upper decks united at the point of delivery, No 320 was one complete unit. Its frames were constructed in steel onto which were riveted aluminium panels with the exception of the front dashes, which were again constructed in steel. The segregated driver's cab projected at both ends and was provided with a seat; the tapering was designed to cope with possible overhang problems on sharp curves. With passenger flow in mind, the tram was designed with rear entrance and front exit with a straight staircase at either end. The air-operated exit doors were operated by the driver. In all the tram was 40ft 11½in in length, 7ft 3¼in in width – the widest tram operated by MET – and 15ft 0¼in in height; it was thus longer, wider and lower than the majority of the MET fleet. The tram was provided with two equal-wheel maximum traction bogies – again constructed by UCC – that owed much to prevailing Underground practice and thus presumably the direct influence of Graff-Baker – which were fitted with two MV101 35hp motors each. Controllers were two English Electric DB2s. Although never required in practice, one truck was equipped with a plough for use on the conduit system. Seating accommodation was provided for sixty-two: twenty-two on the lower and forty on the upper deck.

Nicknamed 'Blossom', No 320 went into service on route 40 – Cricklewood to Whetstone – in May 1929 but the unusual bogies proved problematic with the result that a pair of replacement bogies was constructed at Hendon; these were heavier than the original pair and the weight of the tram increased as a consequence by more than a ton to just over 18 tons.

With the creation of the LPTB in July 1933, No 320 was renumbered 2166. With the conversion of the 40 on 2 August 1936, the tram was withdrawn. Although thought was given to its transfer – with replacement trucks – to south London, this was not progressed and No 2166 was scrapped in early 1937.

The second experimental 'Feltham' – No 330 – is pictured outside Fulwell depot when new and prior to delivery to MET. (London Transport/Barry Cross Collection/Online Transport Archive)

When introduced to service on 6 November 1929, No 330 commenced operation with the conductor seated and using a National ticket-issuing machine. However, experience on the outward journey from Finchley to Golders Green, which demonstrated the impracticality of pay as you enter operation with graduated fares on a busy route, resulted in the conductor reverting to traditional methods for the return journey and the abandonment of the PAYE system. (London Transport/Barry Cross Collection/Online Transport Archive)

22 • THE LONDON FELTHAM TRAM

The rear platform of No 330; the doors were of the top-hung folding style – similar to those fitted to No 320 – but fitted to step level to prevent passengers gaining a foothold when the doors were closed. Designed for PAYE operation, the platform was configured to permit the conductor to sit immediately to the left of the entrance with access to the upper deck being gained via the reversed staircase. (London Transport/Barry Cross Collection/Online Transport Archive)

The front exit door of No 330; this was slightly different to that fitted to No 320 and comprised a single air-worked sliding door. As with the rear entrance doors, the door included a section that dropped down to step level to prevent use of the steps as a foothold once the door was closed. (London Transport/Barry Cross Collection/Online Transport Archive)

Constructed alongside No 320, No 330 was, however, not destined to enter service until November 1929. This was the consequence of the decision to seek alternative control equipment; at the time, this was only available through the American General Electric Co – the owner of BTH – and there were problems in developing the equipment to a form that satisfied Graff-Baker. This was only resolved during the late summer and early autumn of 1929, with the result that it was not until late September that the car made its first test runs.

Externally, the tram was virtually identical to No 320; in construction terms the only significant changes were the use of aluminium panels rather than steel for the front dashes – this was a means of saving some weight – and slight modification to the doors. The maximum traction bogies were supplied by Brush and were fitted with two BTH 509 35hp motors each allied to BTHB527B controllers. Internally, the major difference was that No 330 was designed for PAYE operation; this meant that the staircases were reversed and ticket-issuing equipment was installed for

THE EXPERIMENTAL CARS • 23

the conductor on each vestibule. The tram provided accommodation for sixty-eight seated passengers: forty on the upper and twenty-eight on the lower deck.

As with No 320, No 330 was allocated to route 40; however, its first run when entering service on 6 November 1929 demonstrated that the PAYE equipment was unsuitable when handling large numbers of passengers; on the return journey the conductor reverted to normal practice and the PAYE experiment was abandoned.

Following the conversion of route 40 to trolleybus operation in August 1936, No 2167 was transferred to Wood Green for operation on the 39A – as seen here – prior to its transfer south of the river in May 1938.
(Barry Cross Collection/Online Transport Archive)

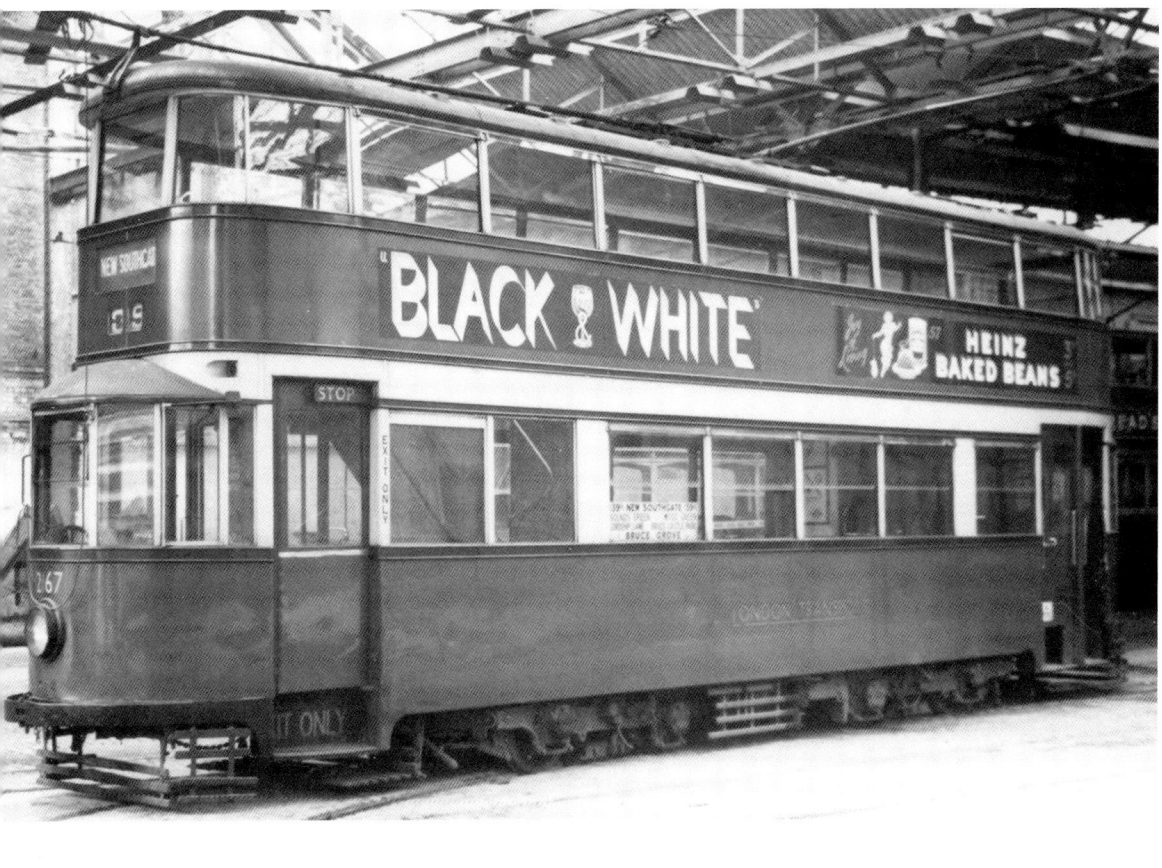

Pictured inside Wood Green depot is No 2167 showing to good effect the reversed staircases that were a necessary feature of its design for PAYE operation. Note also the 'STOP' sign above the front exit; this was an additional safety feature required by the Ministry of Transport to emphasise to other road users that passengers were exiting the tram from the front. (W.A. Camwell/National Tramway Museum)

Seen prior to its transfer south of the river, No 2167 was the only one of the experimental 'Felthams' to see service in London post-war. It was withdrawn and scrapped during 1949. (D.W.K. Jones/National Tramway Museum)

THE EXPERIMENTAL CARS • 25

MET No 331 as completed. The driver's cab was slightly higher than that provided on Nos 320 and 330; the seated driver's eyeline was, therefore, set at the same height as that of a standing driver on older cars and thus the use of standard height controllers was permitted. (Barry Cross Collection/Online Transport Archive)

At the creation of the LPTB, No 330 was renumbered 2167. It remained allocated to Finchley depot until the conversion of the 40 on 2 August 1936. It then spent two years based at Wood Green until 8 May 1938 and the conversion of the 39A when it was transferred south of the river. Of all the experimental trams that led to the 'Feltham' class, No 2167 was the only one that survived to see operation in London after the Second World War.

Although both Nos 320 and 330 had been completed with entrance and exit doors at the platform ends, Spencer – still influenced by his travels in the early 1920s and by contemporary practice elsewhere in the world – was still keen on the concept of constructing a centre-entrance tram and he obtained permission to construct the future No 331 at the same time as the go-ahead was given to purchase the production cars.

As completed in December 1930, No 331 was similar in construction to the earlier experimental cars, being largely completed with aluminium panels with steel dashes. The doors were opened by the driver but were closed by the conductor through the use of push buttons. When constructed, the central vestibule incorporated a combined ticket machine and cash register, but this was removed before the tram entered service. Seating accommodation was provided for twenty-eight – longitudinal seating split between the two saloons – on the lower deck and forty-two on the upper. Access to the upper deck was via two straight staircases located on either side of the central entrances. The tram was equipped with

The upper deck of MET No 331 when new. Accommodation was provided for forty-two passengers with the seats being upholstered in dark blue leather. (London Transport/D.W.K. Jones Collection/Online Transport Archive)

In contrast to the dark blue seats on the upper deck of No 331, those on the lower were upholstered in blue-grey moquette. A total of twenty-eight passengers could be seated, fourteen in each saloon. (London Transport/D.W.K. Jones Collection/Online Transport Archive)

THE EXPERIMENTAL CARS • 27

equal-wheel bogies, built at Hendon and originally scheduled for use under No 330, each fitted with two GEC WT18 35hp motors operated by BTH B49 controllers. No 331 was completed in a non-standard livery with the centre panelling being completed in red rather than the usual ivory.

Following testing from LUT's Fulwell depot, No 331 was based at Finchley depot and entered service on route 40 between Cricklewood and Whetstone in late 1930. Used heavily on peak hour services (in particular the short working between Golders Green and North Finchley), operational experience dictated that two conductors – one for each deck – were normally required. The use of a crew of three was not cost-effective with only 70 passengers.

Slightly modified during its relatively short life in London, No 331 became LPTB No 2168 in July 1933 and was taken out of service and stored on 2 August 1936 following the conversion of the 40 to trolleybus operation. In January 1937, the tram was sold to Sunderland Corporation and transferred to Wearside.

There are only a limited number of known photographs of ex-MET No 331 in service with the LPTB carrying its post-1933 number. Photographed at North Finchley, this view records No 2168 operating on route 45. Sold to Sunderland in 1937, No 2168 would see the bulk of its working life on Wearside before preservation. Note the 'Centre Exit' warning on the front dash and the split 'London Transport' legend along the side. No 2168 was unique in displaying the fleet name in this way. (Marcus Gaywood via Barry Cross Collection/Online Transport Archive)

CONSTRUCTION AND DEVELOPMENT

The decision to give the go-ahead for the construction of the production 'Feltham' cars was tied into the negotiations between LUT and MET with Middlesex County Council over an extension to the operators' leases to the track owned by the council. The council was keen to see replacement trams in use but the companies' financial position was not strong. However, negotiations proceeded and during 1930 it was agreed that a total of 101 cars would be purchased from the Union Construction & Finance Co. Of these, fifty-five – including the one-off No 331 – would be destined for MET with the remaining forty-six allocated to LUT. The total cost, including modification to Finchley depot, came to £198,250 for the MET. Of the LUT fleet, the total cost for the forty-six cars was £150,694 of which £4,444 was for the non-standard 46th car – LUT No 396 – which was to be fitted with English Electric, rather than GEC, equipment. Formal approval for the order was given on 3 April 1930 and announced officially in August the same year. The first deliveries were scheduled for December 1930.

The bodies were constructed of welded steel framing with mild steel panelling on

LUT No 358 is pictured at Hanwell depot in about January 1931 shortly after its completion. This was to become LPTB No 2127 and, following transfer to the West Riding, Leeds No 568. One of the last 'Felthams' to re-enter service, No 568's second career was to be relatively short. (Barry Cross Collection/Online Transport Archive)

the lower decks and aluminium panelling on the upper, with the twin staircases forming an integral part of the framework. On completion of each bodyshell at Feltham, it was transported to Fulwell depot on a low-loader for the completion of electrical and mechanical work. Apart from the fitting of ploughs on the MET cars – which was handled at Hendon – all work was completed at Fulwell.

Each of the production cars was 40ft 6in in length with a width of 7ft 1¾in and a height from track to trolley plank of 15ft 2½in. The total unladen weight of each car – without the plough gear – was 18 tons 6 cwt. Seating capacity was sixty-four – twenty-two on the lower deck and forty-two on the upper – with an additional ten spaces for standing passengers in the vestibule; in terms of seats, this was slightly fewer than carried on the standard 'E/1' type (73). One facility that passengers would have enjoyed was the fact that – unusually for the time – heating was provided.

In order to accommodate a seated – rather than standing – driver, the driver's compartment was raised by 11¾in from that on Nos 320 and 330. Access to the cab was via a hinged door to the rear of the cab; when the driver's seat was lowered, a bolt was engaged that prevented the door being opened. Initially, the middle section of the windscreen was left unglazed in order to fulfil the Metropolitan Police's requirements; this meant that drivers had to wear protective clothing. The regulations were changed prior to the completion of the MET batch of 'Felthams' and the later deliveries were completed with two-piece hinged windscreens; the earlier cars were quickly modified.

When originally designed, the 'Felthams' fell foul of the Metropolitan Police's regulations regarding the operation of Hackney carriages. This meant that when first delivered, part of the front windscreen – as evinced by this view of MET No 321 when new – had to be open to the elements and the driver thus had to wear protective clothing. Shortly after the introduction of the type, the regulations changed and it became possible to have fully-enclosed driving compartments. As a result, later deliveries had a two-piece windscreen and the earlier examples were modified.
(Real Photographs)

In terms of the equipment, all – bar No 396 – were fitted with maximum traction bogies supplied by EMB. Each of these bogies had a wheelbase of 4ft 6in, primary wheels having a 28in diameter and the pony wheels being 22in. Each bogie was fitted with a single 70hp 509P1 motor supplied by BTH and OK33B controllers in the case of the cars supplied to MET; the LUT cars received GEC WT29 60hp motors and GEC KB5 controllers. Braking was provided by a track brake (in the form of a combined magnetic and rheostatic unit) as well as a handbrake and air-wheel brake. Located on each platform was a supplementary air-brake valve for use in an emergency by either the conductor or a passenger.

The 'Felthams' entered service in the traditional livery with an ivory centre panel between the two decks in contrast to the non-standard livery used on No 331.

Internally, the cars were completed in blue rexine panelling with white ceilings. The lower-deck – tranverse rather than the longitudinal on No 331 – seating was generally in green moquette although a handful of MET cars had grey moquette instead; the upper-deck seating, again transverse, was covered in red rexine.

There had been an issue in service with the front exit of the trams. Confusion was caused to other road users and the Ministry of Transport sought an additional indicator to supplement the light at the rear of the tram. Various experiments were undertaken but none proved adequate until July 1929 when a prototype 'STOP' signal was developed by Philip Pugh, who was employed by MET, and fitted to MET No 329. Following a demonstration at Wood Green depot, the device was approved and, slightly modified, was fitted to all the 'Felthams' supplied to

The last LUT 'Feltham' to be completed – No 396 – was non-standard. It was fitted with experimental equal-wheel bogies, DK131 motors and carden shaft drive with worm-geared finials as well as English Electric CBB2 Form 5 controllers. All of this equipment was removed in about 1937 with replacement trucks from No 2317 and BTH B49 controllers reused from withdrawn ex-MET 'H' class car No 2248. (Charles Klapper/copyright The Bus Archive)

One of the experimental equal-wheel bogies supplied by English Electric, fitted with magnetic brakes, for use on LUT No 396. As No 2165, the 'Feltham' was withdrawn post-war following an accident and was scrapped at Purley depot in December 1949. (D.W.K. Jones Collection/Online Transport Archive)

LUT and MET. (Operationally, during the later years with the LPTB, use of the front exit declined and all passengers – either getting on or off – made use of the rear platform with the front exit being employed by the driver as a short cut to or from the driver's cab.)

The last LUT 'Feltham' to be built, No 396, was completed using English Electric supplied 'Liverpool pattern' equal-wheel monomotor frame-less bogies. This car was budgeted to cost £4,444, almost £1,200 more than the GEC-equipped cars (which were costed at £3,250 each). The tram was also initially fitted with English Electric DK120 motors, but these were replaced by the same manufacturer's DK131 motors by early 1932. As in Liverpool, the monomotor bogies were deemed unsuccessful and were replaced by maximum-traction bogies built at Hendon by 1935. The DK131 motors were replaced by the BTH 510AS motors previously used on No 350 (by now LPTB No 2317); the latter car, which had been taken out of service following the conversion of route 57 to trolleybus operation on 27 October 1935, was then scrapped at Hendon.

The experimental car MET No 139 *Poppy* – later LUT No 350 – was to survive to become LPTB No 2317 in July 1933. Seen here with its new fleet name and number, but still in LUT livery, No 2317 was eventually to be repainted into LPTB livery but was not to survive long in the new ownership. Operating on route 57, between Hounslow and Shepherd's Bush, it was withdrawn from service and scrapped following that service's conversion to trolleybus operation on 27 October 1935. Pictured following its withdrawal, No 2317 has lost its bogies and motors prior to scrapping at Hendon. The latter were transferred to the last LUT 'Feltham' to enter service – No 396 (LPTB No 2165) – in place of the latter's non-standard English Electric DK131 motors. (Barry Cross Collection/Online Transport Archive)

CONSTRUCTION AND DEVELOPMENT • 33

EARLY YEARS OF SERVICE

Prior to the entry into service of the 'Felthams', a series of comparative trials were held on Christmas Day 1930 between Enfield Town and Ponders End on the MET system. The tests, designed to indicate the variations in performance between the BTH-fitted trams supplied to MET as opposed to the GEC-fitted examples acquired by LUT, demonstrated that the GEC equipment supplied to LUT was ideal for its type of service – routes with longer intervals between stops and quieter traffic conditions.

The first LUT cars to enter service did so on 5 January 1931 on route 7 from Shepherd's Bush to Uxbridge. It had been proposed in late 1929 that this route would have been reconstructed partially on reserved sleeper track; this work was, however, never undertaken and this resulted in the potential offered by the new trams was never fully exploited.

Initially, eight cars were available, which meant that the service had to be supplemented by some of the fleet's older cars. Although the class was tested on the route from Hampton Court to Kingston, route 7 was to become the type's regular haunt as the length of the new trams – 40ft 3¾in – made the curves on the other routes too tight. It is possible – although there is no photographic evidence to prove the case – that the type also operated on route 55 from Brentford to Hanwell.

Even before the creation of the LPTB, there was a threat to the future of the LUT system; under the terms of the London United Tramways Act of August 1930, the company was empowered to operate trolleybuses over the bulk of its network and work soon started on the erection of trolleybus overhead between Teddington and Twickenham. Trolleybus operation by LUT commenced on 16 May 1931.

With a policeman on point duty in the foreground, an LUT 'Feltham' stands at the terminus of route 7 at Shepherd's Bush on 16 September 1931. The 7 was a heavy trunk route and passenger loadings increased following the introduction of the 'Feltham' class to the route. (Barry Cross Collection/Online Transport Archive)

LUT No 365 pictured at Shepherd's Bush. This car was destined to become LPTB No 2134 and, following withdrawal in April 1951 and transfer to the West Riding, Leeds No 566. Not entering service in Leeds until March 1955, the car survived until being scrapped in April 1959. (Barry Cross Collection/Online Transport Archive)

An LUT 'Feltham' is seen in Ealing Broadway with an inbound service towards Shepherd's Bush on route 7. Note the original warning with lamp on the front; a similar warning on the rear was used to indicate to other road users that passengers also alighted from the front of the tram. Following concerns expressed by the Ministry of Transport, this warning was supplemented by an arm that came out from the side to reinforce the message that passengers made use of the front of the vehicle to exit the tram; the arm was small and unimposing, and was probably missed by most other road users. (Barry Cross Collection/Online Transport Archive)

EARLY YEARS OF SERVICE • 35

Recorded in about 1931, LUT No 382 has suffered damage following a collision; repaired and returned to service, the tram was to become LPTB No 2151. This was one of the ex-LUT cars that were sold to Leeds but never entered service in the West Riding. Notionally allocated the Leeds No 576, it was to be scrapped during the summer of 1956 whilst retaining its London livery and fleet number.
(D.W.K. Jones/National Tramway Museum)

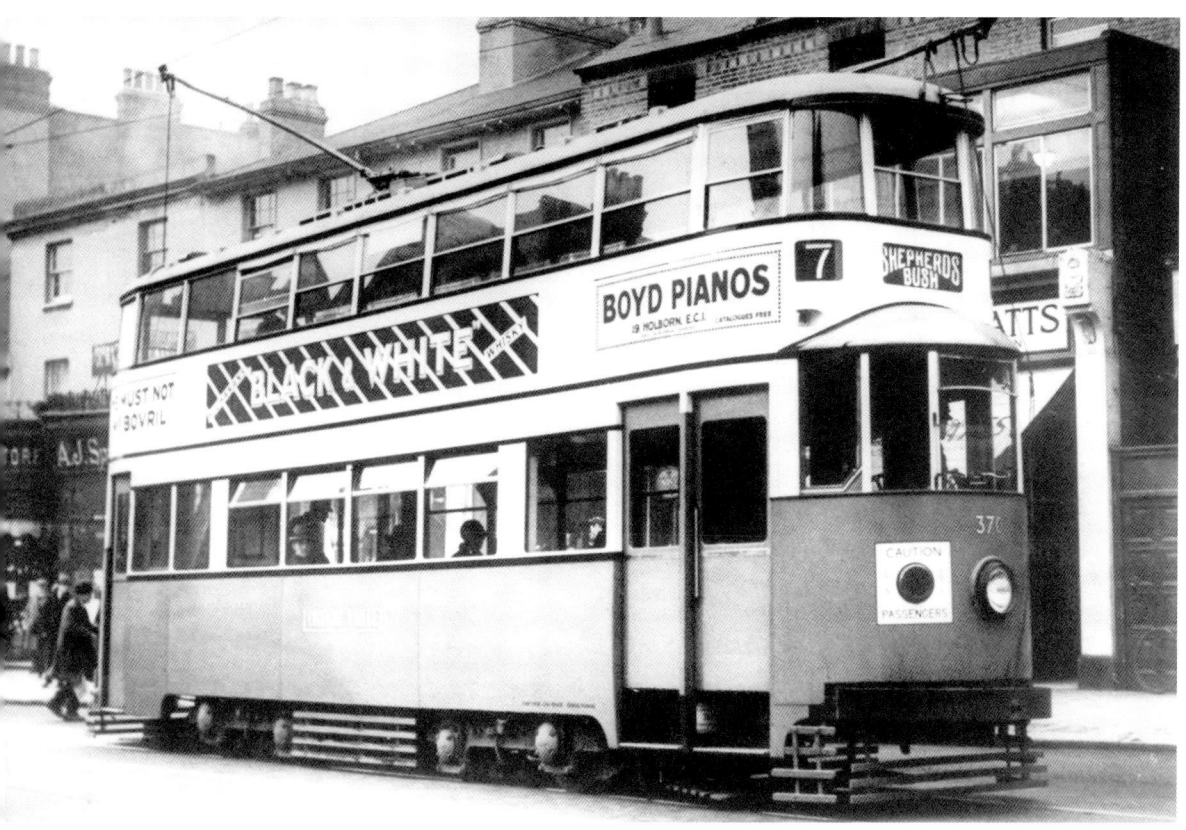

LUT No 370 pictured on route 7 when virtually brand new; this was to become LPTB No 2139 and Leeds No 551 when it entered service – the first of the ex-LUT cars to do so in the West Riding – on 31 October 1951. (D.W.K. Jones/National Tramway Museum)

MET Nos 344 (on route 21) and 291 (on route 59) await departure from the Holborn terminus on Grays Inn Road. The 'Feltham' would become LPTB No 2088 in 1933 and Leeds Corporation No 512 in 1951. It was one of the trams that survived through to the final closure of the system in November 1959. Ex-MET route No 21 was one of those converted to trolleybus operation – as route 521 – on 6 March 1938. The treatment of the windows on the upper and lower deck varied; on the former, the upper sections were designed to wind down but the windows on the lower were hinged. (J. Joyce Collection/Online Transport Archive)

EARLY YEARS OF SERVICE • 37

Operation of the LUT 'Felthams' on route 7 continued until the service was converted to trolleybus operation on 15 November 1936. The trams were then fitted with plough carriers – as built they were not fitted with this equipment but provision was made for its addition if required – following their removal from Hanwell depot to Hampstead before being transferred south of the river to Brixton Hill and Telford Avenue depots.

The results of the tests held in December 1930 also demonstrated that the BTH equipment supplied for use on the MET cars – designed for use on heavily trafficked routes with frequent stops – was again ideal for the MET services over which the type was planned to operate and the first MET 'Felthams' to enter service did so on 1 February 1931 when they appeared on the route from Cricklewood to Whetstone (the 40). Although one car experimentally ran through to Barnet church in order to test clearances, a sharp curve at the bottom of Barnet Hill was such as to prevent operation of the 'Felthams' between Whetstone and Barnet. As more were delivered, operation was extended to route 21 from Holborn to North Finchley.

The final MET 'Feltham' was delivered in late October 1931; by this date, Nos 355-75 were allocated to Finchley depot – where all were initially sent on delivery – with the remainder based at Wood Green. With delivery complete, operation commenced on the joint route 29 – from Enfield to Tottenham Court Road – alongside 'E/1' cars supplied by the LCC.

Pictured at the Uxbridge terminus of route 7 to Shepherd's Bush is LUT No 356. This service was to be converted to trolleybus operation – as route 607 – on 15 November 1936. No 356 was to become LPTB No 2100 and subsequently Leeds Corporation No 513. It survived through in the West Riding until withdrawal in December 1957. The tram was not scrapped, however, until April 1959. (J. Joyce Collection/Online Transport Archive)

WOODHOUSE ROAD, NORTH FINCHLEY.

MET No 326 is pictured at Woodhouse Road, North Finchley, with a service on route 21. No 326 was destined to become LPTB No 2072 in July 1933. (Barry Cross Collection/Online Transport Archive)

The last two MET routes operated by the 'Felthams' were the 29 and 39A and, when these routes were converted on 8 May 1938, the class was transferred south of the river to Telford Avenue. No 354, seen here on the 29, was to become LPTB No 2098 and was to remain in service until January 1951. It was to become Leeds No 542 later the same year and was one of the class that survived through until the end of the Leeds system in November 1959. (Jack Law Collection/Online Transport Archive)

EARLY YEARS OF SERVICE • 39

MET No 348 (Later LPTB No 2092 and Leeds Corporation No 533) is pictured in Enfield. Route 29 was jointly operated with the LCC, but the latter's 'E/1' class struggled to match the performance of the more powerful 'Felthams' on the service. Note that the driver has his summer white top on his cap.
(Maurice O'Connor/National Tramway Museum)

MET No 329 seen outside Wood Green depot. Initial deliveries of 'Felthams' to MET were to Finchley depot but by late 1931 Nos 319/21-54 were allocated to Wood Green with the remainder still based at Finchley. No 329 was to become LPTB No 2071 and Leeds Corporation No 530. The 'Feltham' cars were fitted with two trolleypoles as clearly evinced in this view. (Barry Cross Collection/Online Transport Archive)

Two 'Felthams' stand at Wood Green awaiting departure; closest to the camera is No 327 on route 29 towards Tottenham Court Road. The car behind is on route 21 towards Holborn. The 29 was a joint service with the LCC and an LCC car can be seen on the extreme left heading north towards Winchmore Hill. (C. Carter/Online Transport Archive)

MET No 360 – subsequently LPTB No 2104 – is pictured at Market Parade, North Finchley, with an inbound service on route 21 towards Holborn. The service ran from North Finchley via New Southgate, Wood Green, Manor House, Finsbury Park and King's Cross.
(D.W.K. Jones Collection/ Online Transport Archive)

The decision to convert the erstwhile MET network to trolleybus operation meant that the future of the 'Feltham' in north London was limited. The first of the 'Feltham' operated routes to pass to trolleybus operation was the 40 – by the date of conversion renumbered as route 45 – which succumbed finally on 3 August 1936 (having been reduced as a result of conversions undertaken on 5 July 1936). The conversion of the 45 permitted the transfer of the 'Felthams' to route 39A (from Bruce Grove to Enfield).

'Feltham' operation in north London was finally to cease during 1938 when the remainder of the ex-MET system was converted to trolleybus operation. On 6 March of that year, two of the 'Feltham' operated routes were affected; these were the 21, which was replaced by trolleybus services 521 and 621, and the 39A, which was abandoned without replacement. This resulted in the transfer of the 'Felthams' used on these routes and based at Finchley depot to south London; Finchley depot was closed to trams at the same time. Two months later, on 8 May, the last 'Feltham' operated route – the 29 – was converted. This resulted in the 'Felthams' allocated to Wood Green depot following those previously allocated to Finchley south of the river. The last of the 'Felthams' to leave north London was No 2077, which was delayed slightly whilst repairs to slight damage caused by an accident were undertaken. The transfer of the 'Felthams' saw the cars traverse, unusually, the Kingsway subway.

Seen at the terminus at Uxbridge, shortly after the take over by the LTPB in July 1933, No 2163 has been renumbered but still retains its LUT livery. No 2163 – ex-LUT No 394 – was one of a handful of the class to be withdrawn before the wholesale withdrawal of the type. (J. Joyce Collection/Online Transport Archive)

EARLY YEARS OF SERVICE • 43

By now repainted into LPTB livery as No 2135, ex-LUT No 366 is seen on route 7 shortly before its conversion to trolleybus operation. Note the modified warning sign and lamp on the front panel. (Barry Cross Collection/Online Transport Archive)

Ex-MET route No 21 ran from Holborn to North Finchley via King's Cross, Caledonian Road, Finsbury Park, Manor House, Wood Green and New Southgate. It was one of the routes converted to trolleybus operation on 6 March 1938. Appropriately an ex-MET 'Feltham' but now renumbered and repainted, stands at the Holborn terminus with a northbound service. (Jack Law Collection/Online Transport Archive)

44 • THE LONDON FELTHAM TRAM

Recorded at the Holborn terminus of route 21 is No 2074. This had originally been MET No 328 and was to survive until withdrawal in September 1950. Transferred to Leeds, as No 510, the car was finally withdrawn in March 1959.
(W.J. Wyse Collection/LRTA (London Area) Collection/Online Transport Archive)

No 2069 – ex-MET No 323 – stands at the terminus of route 29 in Enfield. This was destined to be the last 'Feltham' operated route in north London when it was converted to trolleybus operation on 8 May 1938.
(W.J. Wyse Collection/LRTA (London Area) Collection/Online Transport Archive)

EARLY YEARS OF SERVICE • 45

Also seen in Enfield is No 2101; this had originally been MET No 357. Withdrawn in January 1951, the tram was to re-enter service as Leeds No 546 later in the same year. Final withdrawal occurred in May 1959. (W.J. Wyse Collection/LRTA (London Area) Collection/Online Transport Archive)

Standing next to a somewhat battered No 2272 is No 2077. The 'Feltham' had originally been MET No 333 and was one of the earliest to be transferred to Leeds. Withdrawn in August 1950, it became Leeds No 503 when it re-entered service two months later. No 2272 was one of twenty Class G trams – MET Nos 217-36 (LT Nos 2262-81) – built at Hendon Works as open-top cars in 1909. By 1929 all had been rebuilt with enclosed upper decks and, by the creation of the LPTB, they had also received lower-deck windscreens. No 2272 was to be scrapped in June 1938. (W.A. Camwell/National Tramway Museum)

Pictured inside Wood Green depot is No 2066 with, in the background, two of the 15 Class F single-deck trams – Nos 2302 and 2312 – that passed to the LPTB from the MET. The twenty cars of Class F were the only single-deck trams owned by the MET and five had been sold to New Zealand prior to the creation of the LPTB. They were designed for use on the route to Alexandra Palace and for those routes where low railway bridges precluded the use of double-deck trams. The surviving cars were all withdrawn on 23 February 1938 following the closure of the Alexandra Palace route. No 2066 was – as No 319 – numerically the first of the production batch of 'Felthams' supplied to the MET. Withdrawn in September 1950, it was to become Leeds No 506 when it re-entered service two months later. It was to survive through until May 1959. (Barry Cross Collection/Online Transport Archive)

A second view of Wood Green depot sees ex-MET 'Felthams', from left to right, Nos 2084, 2104 and 2073, awaiting their next duties alongside a further Class F single-decker No 2303 and ex-Met Class C/1 No 2294 (on the extreme left). The twenty cars that comprised Class C/1 – Nos 2282-2301 – differed from the fifteen Class C/2s in being fitted with M&G reversed maximum traction bogies rather than Brush BB bogies. Originally delivered during 1907 and 1908 as open-top cars, all were fitted with enclosed top covers before the creation of the LPTB. All thirty-five were to be withdrawn during 1936 and 1937 as the ex-MET network was converted to trolleybus operation. All three of the 'Felthams' were to see further service following withdrawal by the LTE in Leeds. (W.A. Camwell/National Tramway Museum)

Recorded outside Wood Green depot, which was undergoing reconstruction for trolleybus operation at the time, is No 2080; this had originally been MET No 336 and was to become Leeds No 516 when re-entering service in the West Riding in 1951. Note the horse-drawn tower wagon visible beyond the tram in the depot. (Barry Cross Collection/Online Transport Archive)

Recorded heading northwards from the Holborn terminus of route 21 is No 2114. This had originally been MET No 370 and was destined to survive in service with the LPTB until January 1951. Behind is ex-LCC 'E/1' No 533 on route 3; this service linked Holborn with Hampstead via King's Cross and Kentish Town. Route 3 was to be replaced by trolleybus services 513/613 on 10 July 1938. By that date, tram services on route 21 had already been converted to trolleybus operation; this took place on 6 March 1938. (D.W.K. Jones Collection/Online Transport Archive)

No 2076 is seen at the Tottenham Court Road terminus of route 29 to Enfield. This service had been operated jointly between the MET and the LCC prior to the creation of the LPTB and ran via Camden Town, Finsbury Road, Manor House, Wood Green and Winchmore Hill. No 2076 had originally been MET No 332 and, following withdrawal in September 1950, was to become Leeds No 524. (W.A. Camwell/National Tramway Museum)

EARLY YEARS OF SERVICE • 49

Also withdrawn during September 1950 was No 2081; it is seen here at the Enfield terminus of route 29 towards the end of the type's life in north London. The 29 was to be converted to trolleybus operation on 8 May 1938.
(W.A. Camwell/National Tramway Museum)

Pictured receiving the attention of the cleaners is No 2109; this had originally been MET No 365 and was destined to be one of two of the type to be lost as a result of enemy action during the Second World War. It was destroyed at Kennington Gate on 24 August 1944.
(D.W.K. Jones Collection/Online Transport Archive)

50 • THE LONDON FELTHAM TRAM

Ex-MET route 40 linked Cricklewood with North Finchley via Golders Green. Prior to the route's conversion to trolleybus operation – on 3 August 1936 – the service had been renumbered 45; this and a number of other revisions to the route numbering system took effect with the introduction of the winter schedule on 3 October 1934. No 2107 – ex-MET 363 – is seen on the short-lived route 45.
(D.W.K. Jones/National Tramway Museum)

No 2112 – ex-MET No 368 – is seen here at Kingsway, North Finchley, with a service towards Cricklewood during the period when the service was numbered 45. No 2112 was to become Leeds No 547 when it re-entered service in the West Riding in July 1951, six months after its withdrawal in the Metropolis.
(D.W.K. Jones Collection/Online Transport Archive)

EARLY YEARS OF SERVICE • 51

Pictured at the terminus of route 21 at Holborn with a second 'Feltham' in the distance is No 2068. This had originally been MET No 322 and was to survive in LT service until January 1951. Becoming Leeds No 539, the tram was to remain in service in the West Riding until the end of the Leeds system. (D.W.K. Jones Collection/Online Transport Archive)

Following its transfer to south London, No 2134 is seen operating on route 8 – the ex-LCC Tooting to Victoria service – over the conduit. Originally LUT No 365, No 2134 was withdrawn in April 1951 and was to enter service in Leeds almost exactly four years later as No 566. (W.J. Wyse Collection/LRTA (London Area) Collection/ Online Transport Archive)

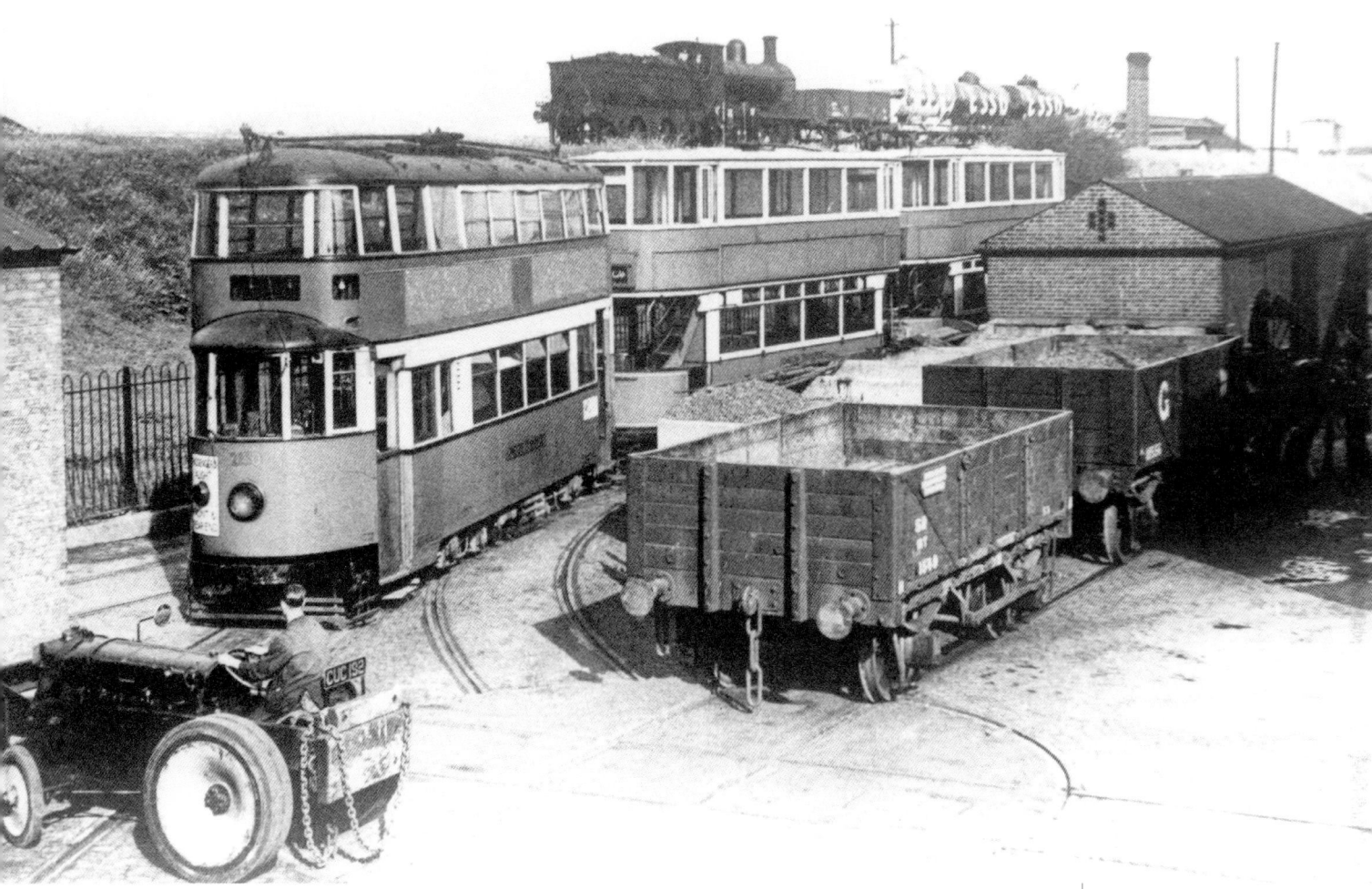

No 2150 is seen at Charlton Works in September 1938 following its transfer south of the river. This had originally been LUT No 381 and was destined, following final withdrawal in London in April 1951, to become Leeds No 553. It was one of the first of the ex-LUT cars to re-enter service and was to survive until September 1957. The transfer of the 'Feltham' cars from north to south of the river required that they pass through the Kingsway Subway, the only physical connection between the routes north and south of the river by the late 1930s. (O. J. Morris/Barry Cross Collection/Online Transport Archive)

LAST YEARS IN LONDON

With the conversion of route 29 in May 1938, all of the 'Feltham' trams were now based south of the River Thames. If World War 2 had not occurred their sojourn south of the river might have been considerably shorter but the outbreak of war in September 1939 meant that the London tram network's life was considerably extended. The 'Felthams' were longer than all the other trams based in south London and, as a result, they could not be easily accommodated. Allocated primarily to Telford Avenue and, to a lesser extent, Brixton Hill, they could be seen on a number of routes operated – such as the 8, 10, 16, 18, 20 and 22 plus all-night services – from these depots.

Although London was not the initial target when the Battle of Britain commenced during the summer of 1940, once the German tactics changed and the city became a major focus for attack, London Transport was to suffer severe damage. The first raid that resulted in significant damage or dislocation to the surviving tram network occurred on 8 September 1940 when a High Explosive bomb landed on Brixton Road. This resulted in the diversion of routes 10, 16, 18 and 33 with the track along Brixton Road being closed until 7 October.

The first 'Feltham' to suffer damage was No 2142. This occurred at about 9am on Friday, 27 September when a High Explosive bomb landed in a garden on South Lambeth Road. The blast blew out the windows on the tram whilst a bush was blown on to the tram's roof. No 2142 was repaired and returned to service.

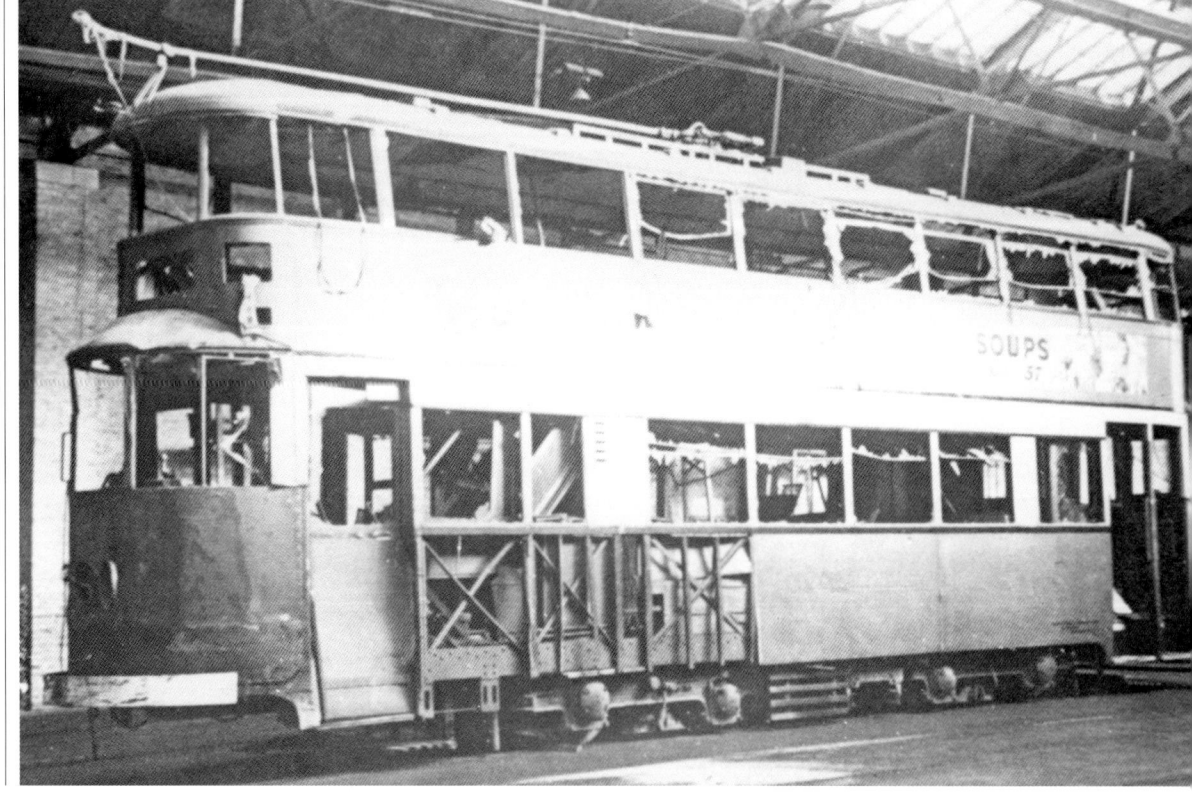

London's tramways were not immune to the destruction wrought by the Luftwaffe during the Second World War and the bombing campaign against the capital. A number of trams including two 'Felthams' (No 2113 on 26 October 1940 and No 2109 on 24 August 1944) – were to be destroyed as a result of enemy action; this view, taken in Brixton Hill depot, is believed to record the damage sustained by No 2113.
(J. Joyce Collection/Online Transport Archive)

54 • THE LONDON FELTHAM TRAM

The first 'Feltham' to be destroyed by enemy action was No 2113, which was hit by a bomb that fell on Stockwell Road during Saturday, 26 October 1940. Bomb damage often resulted in trams operating shuttle services or on diversion; on Sunday, 17 November 1940, for example, four 'Felthams' – Nos 2078/121/130/161 – were employed on a shuttle service between Streatham Library and Tooting. On 16 April 1941, No 2090 was marooned at Brixton station and No 2089 north of Stockwell Road as a result of bomb damage on Brixton Road. By the end of the following month, the Blitz was largely over, although London continued to come under spasmodic attack. This was particularly the case later in the war with the German use of the V1 and V2 flying bombs. It was during one of these raids – on 24 August 1944 – that a second 'Feltham' to be destroyed, No 2109, was destroyed at Kennington Gate.

The war ended with ninety-eight of the production 'Felthams' still in service along with one of the experimental cars – No 2167. Over the next few years, the number in service was reduced to ninety-two, with No 2122 being a victim of a serious collision in 1946 and being broken up in May the following year, whilst Nos 2067/91/130/63/65 as well as prototype car No 2167 were withdrawn during 1949 and scrapped at Purley depot during December 1949. The five production cars were all taken out of service as a result of collision damage.

One of the consequences of the war was the permanent diversion of rush-hour trams on routes 22 and 24 away from Brixton Road. In order to compensate for this, extra trams were allocated to short workings of routes 16 and 18. Ex-LCC cars operated these services showing an 'EX' stencil whilst 'Felthams' generally showed either '16X' or '18X'.

Looking in good external condition despite the effects of six years of war, No 2126 stands outside Telford Avenue depot on 31 March 1946 on a service from the Embankment to Purley. New as LUT No 357, No 2126 was to be withdrawn in April 1951. Stored in Leeds, it was eventually to re-enter service – as No 565 – in February 1955.
(Jack Law Collection/Online Transport Archive)

LAST YEARS IN LONDON • 55

Pictured at Vauxhall Cross on 11 May 1946 are, on the left, No 2077 and, on the right, 'E/1' No 1312. No 2077 had been the last of the ex-MET 'Felthams' transferred to Telford Avenue following the conversion of routes 29 and 39A on 8 May 1938. Its transfer was delayed whilst accident damage was repaired. (Geoffrey Ashwell/Online Transport Archive)

Julian Thompson noted a number of 'Felthams' that were emerging fresh from Charlton Works during 1949 and 1950 as routine maintenance work on the type and other service cars continued. On 17 January he listed No 2160 as having been completed, to be followed on 11 March by No 2121; on 25 April by No 2094; on 1 May by Nos 2087 and 2140; on 19 May 1949 by Nos 2085 and 2124; on 25 June by Nos 2154 and 2159; on 10 July by No 2161; on 31 August by Nos 2097 and 2098; on 9 October by Nos 2101, 2107 and 2142; on 23 November by Nos 2103-05; 19 January by No 2135; on 10 March 1950 by Nos 2132, 2144, 2150 and 2162; on 14 April by Nos 2076, 2102, 2129 and 2144; on 8 May by No 2092; on 11 June by Nos 2156 and 2164; on 12 July by Nos 2119 and 2141; and on 17 August by No 2079.

During the summer of 1949 negotiations were undertaken with Leeds Corporation with a view to the sale of the 'Felthams'. With a deal concluded No 2099 was sent to the West Riding for testing; it left London on 20 September 1949. In all, Leeds Corporation agreed to acquire the 92 surviving 'Felthams' at £500 apiece. As a result of tram reallocations during the summer of 1949 to facilitate the rebuilding of depots to accommodate buses during the final conversion programme, 'Felthams' became a more familiar sight on route 22 and 24. At the start of 1950, all of the surviving 'Felthams' were allocated to Telford Avenue depot. Although barred from other services, the type was permitted to access Charlton Works albeit not in passenger service; this meant that the type would become redundant following Stage 3 of 'Operation Tramaway', as this involved the last routes over which they could operate.

Although No 2167, the second of the experimental cars, spent much of the war, after its transfer to Telford Avenue, in store, it was restored to normal service post-war and is seen here at Thornton Heath Pond on 6 July 1946. (Geoffrey Ashwell/Online Transport Archive)

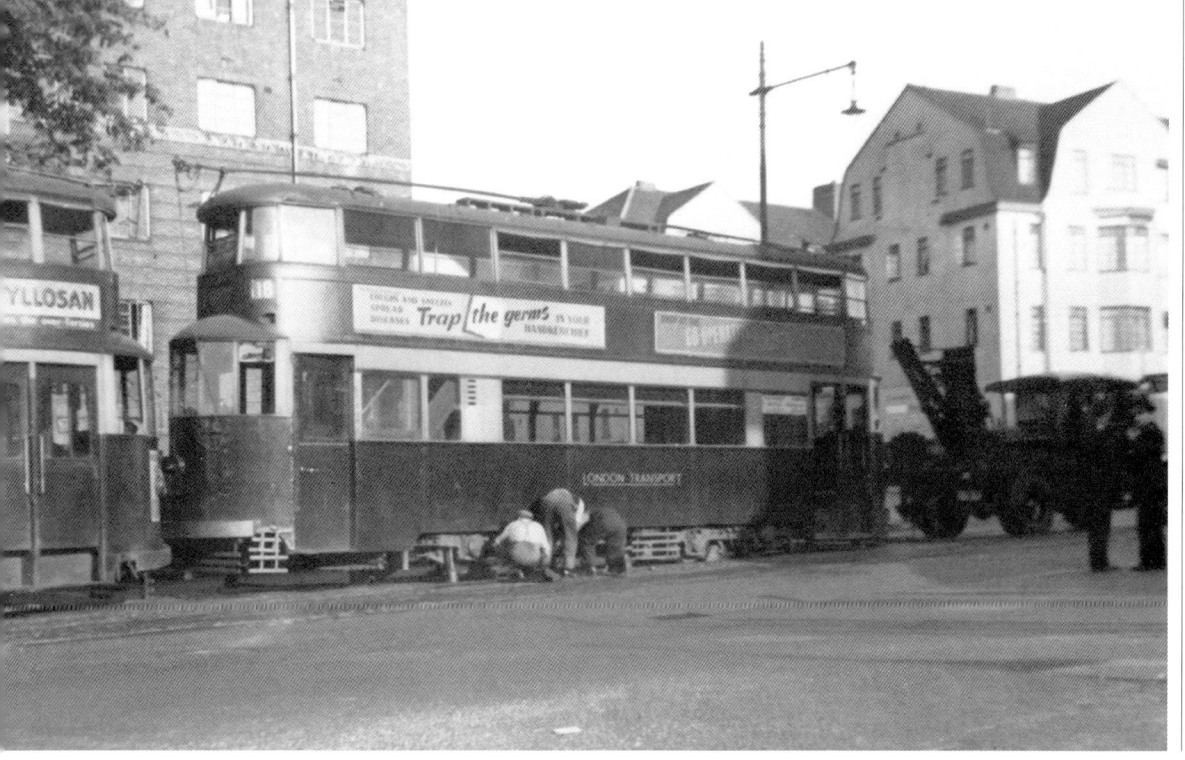

On 25 July 1946, No 2125 is recorded receiving attention on Telford Avenue. This tram was originally LUT No 356 and was to remain in service through until April 1951. It re-entered service in Leeds the following year – as No 561 where it achieved a further seven years' operation. (Geoffrey Ashwell/Online Transport Archive)

LAST YEARS IN LONDON • 57

Pictured on Blackfriars Road are ex-Croydon Corporation No 386 and 'Feltham' No 2100. The ex-Croydon car is heading north towards Blackfriars Bridge and the Embankment whilst No 2100 stands on the terminal stub that stood between the two through running lines. No 2100 was originally MET No 356; withdrawn in September 1950 it became Leeds No 513 when it re-entered service the following year. It was to survive in service until December 1957, being scrapped in April 1959. (Barry Cross Collection/Online Transport Archive)

Heading outbound at Stockwell on route 8 is No 2143. This had originally been LUT No 374 and is pictured alongside Daimler CWA6 No D79 on route 88. The bus was fitted with an austerity Duple body, albeit slightly more comfortable than earlier deliveries, and was new in March 1945. No 2143 was to become Leeds No 581 when it re-entered service in 1952 and was to survive in service until January 1958. (Barry Cross Collection/Online Transport Archive)

58 • THE LONDON FELTHAM TRAM

Three trams – headed by No 2120 – stand at the Victoria terminus on Vauxhall Bridge Road. The 'Feltham' is on route 20 – the service from Victoria via Brixton, Streatham and Tooting back to Victoria – whilst the 'E/1' behind – No 1386 – is on route 78 towards West Norwood. Route 78 was to survive until Stage 6 of 'Operation Tramaway' in January 1952 – long after the withdrawal of the last 'Felthams'. No 2120 was the first of the production batch of LUT 'Felthams' – No 351 – and was to become Leeds No 557 in late 1951. It remained in service in the West Riding until January 1959. (Barry Cross Collection/Online Transport Archive)

Heading inbound across Blackfriars Bridge is No 2105 on a route 18 service towards Croydon and Purley via the Embankment. Note the warning from the City of London Police on the left; although the bulk of the London tramway network was covered by the Metropolitan Police, certain sections approaching the City were under the control of the separate City of London Police. (Barry Cross Collection/Online Transport Archive)

Recorded heading eastbound along Albert Embankment on route 22 towards County Hall is No 2152. This was ex-LUT No 383, which was to become Leeds No 556 in 1951. It remained in service in the West Riding until March 1959. Route 22 was a peak hours only service that linked Savoy Street with Tooting via Clapham; it was to be converted to bus operation as part of Stage 2 of 'Operation Tramaway' in January 1951. (Barry Cross Collection/Online Transport Archive)

In July 1950, Lord Latham, the chairman of the LTE, announced the final conversion programme for the London system. As part of the scheme, an open-air scrapyard was established at Penhall Road, close to Charlton Works, and amongst the first trams to arrive in August 1950 were three 'Felthams' – Nos 2077/82/97 – which had been withdrawn from service prior to being sent north to Leeds. Unlike most trams that made the one-way journey to Penhall Road, however, this trio was destined to head to Yorkshire. The following month a further twenty-six – Nos 2066/69-76/78/80/81/83-88/93/96/100/108/115/116/118/139 – were sent to Penhall Road, again prior to be shipped to the West Riding. They were replaced at Telford Avenue by ex-Leyton Corporation 'E/3s' from Wandsworth. All the 'Felthams' were ex-MET cars by this stage, with the exception of No 2139. By the end of October 1950, six of the 'Felthams' transferred to Penhall Road had been moved to Leeds.

The next two casualties were Nos 2144 and 2162; these were severely damaged in a fire at Brixton depot on 18 October 1950. Their remains were transferred to Penhall Road; deemed irreparable, the two were scrapped with Leeds Corporation taking the unique No 1 in lieu of the two 'Felthams'. A third car – No 2164 – was damaged in the same incident but was repaired and sent to Yorkshire, where it re-entered service (as No 552) in November 1951. The remains of Nos 2144 and 2162 were scrapped at Penhall Road during May 1951. Stage 2 of 'Operation Tramaway' – over the night of 6/7 January 1951 – saw the surviving ex-MET 'Felthams' transferred to Penhall Road.

A second view of a 'Feltham' on route 22 sees No 2147 heading outbound at St Thomas's Hospital with 'E/1' No 1770 following with a service on route 26 towards Clapham Junction. Route 26 was one of the services that was to be converted to bus operation as part of Stage 1 of 'Operation Tramaway' over the weekend of 30 September/ 1 October 1950. (Barry Cross Collection/Online Transport Archive)

Heading south past Streatham Library with a route 18 service towards Croydon and Purley is No 2128. This was new as LUT No 359 and was one of the ex-LUT cars allocated a fleet number – in this case No 572 – but which never re-entered service in Leeds. It was finally scrapped in November 1956. (Barry Cross Collection/Online Transport Archive)

LAST YEARS IN LONDON • 61

Another 'Feltham' allocated a Leeds number but never operated was No 2151, which is seen here in Thornton Heath Pond on route 16. No 2151 was originally LUT No 382; allocated the number 576 by Leeds, it was to be scrapped in July 1956. (Barry Cross Collection/Online Transport Archive)

Standing at the terminus of route 10 on Southwark Bridge is No 2149; this was ex-LUT No 380 and was destined to become Leeds No 580 when it re-entered service in early 1955. Destined for a relatively short life in the West Riding, it was withdrawn during the summer of 1956. Route 10 – from Southwark Bridge to Tooting to Streatham – was another service to be converted to bus operation in January 1951. (Barry Cross Collection/Online Transport Archive)

62 • THE LONDON FELTHAM TRAM

No 2084 stands outside West Croydon station with a southbound service towards Purley. New as MET No 344, No 2084 was withdrawn in September 1950. It re-entered service in Leeds as No 519 the following year and was to survive in service until March 1959, having been renumbered 511 in August 1957. In Leeds No 519 was the subject of an experiment in July 1952 to see if it was possible to convert the car into a single-deck trailer; however, the integral construction of the tram made this impractical and No 519 remained a double-decker until its final withdrawal. (C. Carter/Online Transport Archive)

As the driver checks in his rear-view mirror, passengers board an outbound route 10 car on Mitcham Lane. No 2133 was originally LUT No 364 and was destined to become Leeds No 582 in July 1956 – the last of the ex-LUT cars to enter service in the West Riding. (C. Carter/Online Transport Archive)

Two ex-LUT 'Felthams' are pictured at Kennington with southbound services. In the foreground is No 2157 heading towards Purley whilst No 2132 is travelling only as far as Norbury. The trams were originally LUT Nos 388 and 363 respectively. Both were to survive through to the final withdrawal of the class in April 1951; No 2132 became Leeds No 569 and No 2157 Leeds No 586. (C. Carter/Online Transport Archive)

With the Palace of Westminster in the background, No 2136 crosses Westminster Bridge with a service heading towards the Embankment. Inbound services across the bridge were usually route 18 with route 16 being those cars that headed south over the river at this point. The small corner route number blinds were, unusually, rotated horizontally rather than vertically. (C. Carter/Online Transport Archive)

64 • THE LONDON FELTHAM TRAM

The conductor deals with the trolleypoles on No 2161 as it stands at the terminus in Purley. This had originally been LUT No 392 when new and was to become Leeds No 562 in 1952. (C. Carter/Online Transport Archive)

No 2089 passes Purley depot with an outbound service towards Purley itself. The depot dated originally to 26 September 1901 when it was opened by Croydon Corporation; it lost its tramcar allocation in June 1945 but was used for a period thereafter as a store and, from September 1948, for maintenance work alongside Charlton Works. Until the completion of the 'Tramatorium' at Penhall Road, the depot was also used for the scrapping of trams. In January 1951, following the closure for reconstruction of Telford Avenue, Purley regained an allocation of operational trams for services 16 and 18 prior to their final conversion in April 1951. No 2089 had originally been MET No 345 and, following transfer to Leeds, was to become that operator's No 537. Re-entering service in June 1951, it was to survive until withdrawal in May 1957. (Barry Cross Collection/Online Transport Archive)

No 2147 is seen emerging from Telford Avenue depot. This had originally been LUT No 378; transferred to Leeds in September 1951, it was not until June 1955 that the car re-entered service. Finally withdrawn in January 1959, it was to be scrapped four months later. (Marcus Eavis/Online Transport Archive)

With the Woolworths store in the background, No 2167 heads south along Brixton Road with a service towards Norbury. The tram is showing the 'EX' route number used by certain 'extra' trams running along Brixton Road to Norbury that were introduced when routes 22 and 24 were diverted away from Brixton Road. No 2167 was withdrawn during 1949 and scrapped at Norbury depot in December that year. (F.N.T. Lloyd-Jones/Online Transport Archive)

On 24 April 1948 No 2118 – ex-MET No 374 – is pictured at Mitcham Lane fire station outside St Leonard's Church with a route 10 to Tooting Broadway. Note the panel adjacent to the rear platform; this clearly indicates the change of control following Nationalisation and records the London Transport Executive as the owner. No 2118 was withdrawn in September 1950 and entered service in Leeds as No 517 the following year. Renumbered 554 in February 1959, the tram's operational career came to an end five months later. (John Meredith/Online Transport Archive)

Also recorded on 24 April 1948 whilst operating on route 10, No 2167 – ex- MET No 330 – shows the condition of the second of the two experimental cars towards the end of its life. Transferred to Telford Avenue along with a number of other 'Feltham' cars, No 2167 was little used during the war but was to return to service once hostilities had ceased. No 2167 was to survive in service until late 1949 and was eventually to be scrapped at Purley depot. (John Meredith/Online Transport Archive)

LAST YEARS IN LONDON • 67

Also recorded on 24 April 1948, but this time at the loading island at Woodbourne Avenue on Streatham High Road, is No 2110. This had originally been MET No 366 and was to become one of nineteen of the type withdrawn in January 1951 as a result of Stage 2 of 'Operation Tramaway'. Sent north, it re-entered service as Leeds No 536 later the same year, surviving until withdrawal in December 1958 and scrapping in July 1959. (John Meredith/Online Transport Archive)

Passengers board a route 10 service on Tooting Broadway on 6 June 1949. No 2107 – ex-MET No 363 – was to survive in London until January 1951 and was to re-enter service in Leeds, as No 541, later the same year. (John Meredith/Online Transport Archive)

68 • THE LONDON FELTHAM TRAM

Numerically the highest numbered of the production 'Feltham' cars, No 2165 – ex-LUT No 396 – is seen at Clapham Common on 10 June 1949. This car originally had non-standard experimental equal-wheel bogies with DK131 motors and carden shaft drive with worm-geared finals. This equipment was replaced in about 1937 by trucks with plain axle bearings; these were believed to have been used previously on No 350 (and were the second set of trucks used on that car, being constructed from steel plates by the MET at Hendon). No 396 also originally had non-standard controllers – English Electric CBB2 – but these were later replaced by BTH B49-type controllers from an ex-MET 'H' type (No 2248). No 2165 was seriously damaged in a collision shortly after this photograph was taken and was scrapped at Purley depot in December 1949. (John Meredith/Online Transport Archive)

One of the features of the London tramway system – the change pit – is shown in this view of No 2140 at Streatham on 21 June 1949. No 2140 – ex-LUT No 371 – was to be withdrawn in April 1951. Transferred to Leeds, it was one of seven trams that were refurbished and repainted in Yorkshire but did not immediately re-enter service. As No 563 it emerged in February 1955 and was to survive for a further four years. (John Meredith/Online Transport Archive)

On 5 August 1949 No 2135 is seen heading south on Brixton Hill at its junction with New Park Road. This tram had been new as LUT No 366 and, following withdrawal in April 1951, was transferred to Leeds. Albeit allocated fleet number 584, it never entered service in the West Riding and was scrapped in November 1956. (John Meredith/Online Transport Archive)

Whilst maintenance work is undertaken on the inbound track, No 2082 is seen on London Road, Norbury, with a southbound service on route 18 towards Croydon and Norbury on 13 August 1949. No 2082 was originally MET No 338 and would be withdrawn in August the following year. Becoming Leeds No 504, it re-entered service in October 1950 and was to survive through until final closure of that system in November 1959. (John Meredith/Online Transport Archive)

On 13 August 1949 No 2090 is pictured outside Thornton Heath depot with a northbound service on route 18. The track heading off to the east at this point served route 42 to Thornton Heath. No 2090 had originally been MET No 346 and was to become Leeds Corporation No 544. (John Meredith/Online Transport Archive)

On 27 December 1949 No 2161 – ex-LUT No 392 – is seen on Albert Embankment with a service on route 22. This tram was one of some forty of the type that survived through until April 1951 when, following Stage 3 of 'Operation Tramaway', operation of the type ceased in London. Sent to the West Riding, No 2161 emerged as Leeds No 562 in 1952. After five years' further service, No 562 was withdrawn in August 1956. (John Meredith/Online Transport Archive)

LAST YEARS IN LONDON • 71

As track repair work is undertaken, No 2131 is seen on London Road, Thornton Heath, on 5 February 1950. This car, ex-LUT No 362, was to survive through until April 1951 when all the surviving 'Feltham' cars were withdrawn following Stage 3 of 'Operation Tramaway'. No 2131 was to become Leeds No 555, entering service in the West Riding later in 1951. After almost five years' further service, No 555 was withdrawn in March 1956. (John Meredith/Online Transport Archive)

No 2144 – ex-LUT No 375 – is seen at the Streatham Common crossover on Streatham High Road with a route 18 service on 18 March 1950. No 2144 was one of two destroyed by fire in November 1949 and scrapped at Penhall Road. (John Meredith/Online Transport Archive)

Pictured at the Norbury terminus crossover on Streatham High Road on 19 March 1950 is No 2116 on route 16. This tram was to be withdrawn in September 1950 as a result of Stage 1 of 'Operation Tramaway' and sent north to Leeds, re-entering service in 1951 as No 529. It was to survive in Leeds until the end of the system in November 1959. (John Meredith/Online Transport Archive)

Pictured at Hermitage Bridge, Norbury, on Streatham High Road, No 2123 – ex LUT No 354 – heads towards Purley and Croydon with a service on route 18. This was another of the 'Feltham' cars that was to survive until the end of the type's operation in London, being withdrawn following Stage 3 of 'Operation Tramaway' in April 1951. Sent to Leeds, where it was refurbished and repainted, it was not until March 1955 that the tram re-entered service as Leeds No 564. Final withdrawal was to come in March 1959. (John Meredith/Online Transport Archive)

On 29 May 1950 No 2087 – ex-MET No 343 – is seen at Tooting Junction with a service on route 8. No 2087 was withdrawn four months later and transferred to Leeds. As No 518 it re-entered service in 1951 and was to survive until January 1959. (John Meredith/Online Transport Archive)

The last major trackwork undertaken on the London system involved diversions to cater for the Festival of Britain in 1951. Recorded at Charing Cross on 20 August 1950, No 2093 – ex-MET No 349 – was operating an emergency shuttle service – note the posters in the lower-deck windows – in connection with this work. By this date, No 2093 was approaching the end of its operational life in London; it was to be withdrawn the following month.
(John Meredith/Online Transport Archive)

The work undertaken by the LTE during the summer of 1950 included the construction of a one-way system around County Hall. Pictured using the new track in Addington Street outbound with a route 18 service towards Purley is No 2146. This was new as LUT No 377 and was to become Leeds No 579 in 1952.
(C. Carter/Online Transport Archive)

Seen at the Victoria terminus of the services to Streatham and Tooting – the 8 and the 20 – in 1950 is No 2112. Transferred to Leeds following withdrawal in January 1951, the tram was to enter service in Leeds during the following July as No 547. It was to survive in service in the West Riding for just over six years.
(W.A. Camwell/National Tramway Museum)

LAST YEARS IN LONDON • 75

During the period of the emergency shuttle service – note the poster giving directions in the background – No 2144 is pictured on the Embankment awaiting departure with a route 18 service towards Croydon and Purley. Withdrawn in October 1950, this was one of two 'Felthams' seriously damaged by fire and eventually scrapped at Charlton. It was the loss of this and No 2162 that resulted in ex-LCC No 1 being sent to Leeds as a replacement. (Julian Thompson/Online Transport Archive)

It's 30 September 1950 and as part of the first stage of 'Operation Tramaway' many trams were withdrawn and made their forlorn way to the sidings at Penhall Road, where most were eventually scrapped. However, for No 2072 seen at New Cross Gate the West Riding of Yorkshire beckoned. It re-entered service – as Leeds No 521 – in September 1951 and was to remain in service until March 1959. (John Meredith/Online Transport Archive)

Between Stages 1 and 2 of 'Operation Tramaway', three 'Felthams' were withdrawn as a result of serious fire damage sustained at Brixton depot on 18 November 1950. Although No 2164 was eventually repaired and sent to Leeds, two others – Nos 2144 and 2162 – were more seriously damaged and were to be scrapped at Penhall Road. The sorry remains of these two are visible in this view alongside equally doomed 'E/1' No 1312. (Phil Tatt/Online Transport Archive)

LAST YEARS IN LONDON • 77

Withdrawn 'Felthams' stand in Penhall Road awaiting transfer to Leeds; closest to the camera is No 2088, withdrawn in September 1950, that was to become No 512 in the West Riding. It re-entered service during 1951 and was one of the ex-MET 'Felthams' to survive until the closure of the Leeds system in November 1959. (Harry Luff/Online Transport Archive)

Ex-MET No 2105 is seen departing from Charlton Works for the final time following its withdrawal in September 1950 en route to its new life in the West Riding of Yorkshire. It would emerge as Leeds No 511 the following year and survive through until August 1957. (Barry Cross Collection/Online Transport Archive)

On 11 November 1950 No 2106 is seen on Streatham High Road with a service on route 18X. The '16X' and '18X' services were short workings introduced following the wartime diversion of rush-hour trams on routes 22 and 24 away from Brixton Road. *(John Meredith/Online Transport Archive)*

The peak hours only service 22 – from Savoy Street to Tooting via Streatham – was one of nine tram services affected by Stage 2 of 'Operation Tramaway' in January 1951. Here, No 2143 is seen in Westminster with an outbound service on 18 November 1950. No 2143 had originally been LUT No 374 and was to survive through until April 1951; becoming Leeds No 581 and re-entering service the following year, it was to be one of the longest-surviving ex-LUT cars in Leeds, not been being withdrawn until January 1958 and scrapped in April 1959. *(Julian Thompson/Online Transport Archive)*

By 11 December 1950, when this view of No 2095 was taken on Kennington Park Road, tram operation of route 20 was approaching its final weeks; the service was replaced by buses as part of Stage 2 of 'Operation Tramaway' the following month. No 2095 – ex-MET No 351 – was also to be withdrawn as a result of that conversion. (John Meredith/Online Transport Archive)

Stage 2 of 'Operation Tramaway' occurred on 6/7 January 1951 and saw the elimination of a number of services including route 8 which ran from Victoria via Clapham, Tooting and Streatham back to Victoria (it operated as route 20 in the reverse direction). Pictured at the Lawn Lane crossover on the South Lambeth Road on the last day of tramway operation – 6 January – is ex-LUT No 2161. The tram was to survive for a further three months, being withdrawn in April. Becoming Leeds No 562, it was to remain in service until August 1956; it was scrapped in October 1957. (John Meredith/Online Transport Archive)

80 • THE LONDON FELTHAM TRAM

It's 6 January 1951 and the last day of route 24 – the peak hours only service from Savoy Street to Tooting via Streatham – as No 2102 navigates Albert Embankment, Vauxhall. No 2102 – ex-MET No 358 – was withdrawn as a consequence of Stage 2 of 'Operation Tramaway'. Re-entering service, as No 534, in Leeds later the same year, it was to see more than eight years' service in the West Riding. (John Meredith/Online Transport Archive)

Another casualty of Stage 2 of 'Operation Tramaway' was route 20; this was also a Victoria to Victoria service, this time running via Streatham, Tooting and Clapham. Pictured on the short section of single track at Ramsey Road, Stockwell Road, on 6 January 1951 is No 2128. Note the double conduit section and the opening at Queen's Head pub which had provided access to the former horse tram depot. No 2128 – another ex-LUT car – was also to be withdrawn in April 1951; whilst allocated the fleet number 572 by Leeds Corporation, this was one of the 'Feltham' cars that headed north but was scrapped without entering service. (John Meredith/Online Transport Archive)

Pictured emerging from Telford Avenue depot – before work started on the depot's demolition and rebuilding – on 6 January 1951 is No 2146. Ironically, given the short life expectancy of the tramway system, the poster on the left is advertising vacancies for tram and trolleybus conductors. No 2146 was new as LUT No 377; withdrawn three months after the date of this photograph, the tram was to become Leeds No 579. It re-entered service in 1952 and survived in the West Riding until withdrawal in March 1956 and scrapping in December 1956. (John Meredith/Online Transport Archive)

A busy scene on Telford Avenue on 6 January 1951 sees ex-LUT No 2123 heading south with a service car on an 'extra' to Croydon only whilst behind the car on route 10 as a second 'Feltham' heads north towards the Embankment. No 2123 had originally been LUT No 354 and was to become Leeds No 564. It was to operate in Leeds from March 1955 through to March 1959.
(John Meredith/Online Transport Archive)

82 • THE LONDON FELTHAM TRAM

Pictured near the entrance to the yard at Penhall Road on 6 January 1951, having been withdrawn following Stage 2 of 'Operation Tramway', is No 2079 – ex-MET No 335. However, a mishap to one of the surviving ex-LUT 'Felthams' resulted in No 2079 being restored briefly to passenger service. (J. Joyce Collection/Online Transport Archive)

No 2154 heads north across Westminster Bridge on 21 January 1951 with an inbound service from Purley and Croydon. This tram had originally been LUT No 385; it re-entered service in Leeds – as No 589 – in March 1955 and was finally withdrawn in March 1959. (Julian Thompson)

Recorded at Kennington station, with an outbound service to Croydon and Purley on 18 February 1951, is No 2161. This was new as LUT No 392; transferred to Leeds following withdrawal in April 1951, it re-entered service as No 583 in 1952 and survived until August 1956, being scrapped in October 1957. (Julian Thompson/Online Transport Archive)

Also seen on 18 February 1951, but this time at County Hall, No 2129 is pictured heading inbound with a route 16 service. No 2129 had originally been LUT No 360; transferred to Leeds, it was stored for a period before re-entering service – as No 574 – in June 1956. As such, it was one of the last ex-LUT cars to enter service in Leeds; destined for a relatively short second career, it was withdrawn in March 1959. (Julian Thompson/Online Transport Archive)

With about a month to go before Stage 3 saw the conversion of routes 16, 18 and 42. No 2155 is seen in Brixton Road at its junction with Loughborough Road on 4 March 1951. The pub in the background – then known as The Old White Horse – originally dated to the late eighteenth century, is still extant, albeit with a change of name. No 2155 was new as LUT No 386; transferred to Leeds – and allocated fleet number 571 – it was one of the ex-LUT cars never to operate in the West Riding and was finally disposed of in November 1956. (John Meredith/Online Transport Archive)

Having been taken from Penhall Road and briefly restored to active duty, No 2079 is seen West Croydon on 26 March 1951. (John Meredith/Online Transport Archive)

It's March 1951 and passengers on the top deck of this 'Feltham' are probably aware that it won't be long before they will no longer be able to enjoy travelling on this type of tram. (Jack Law Collection/Online Transport Archive)

No 2085 was the only 'Feltham' to be given a full renovation at Charlton Works after the Second World War, with the work being directed by Vic Matterface who, as the Tramways Rolling Stock Engineer in Leeds, was later instrumental in seeing the surviving 'Felthams' transferred to the West Riding. After the work was completed, the tram was nicknamed the 'Queen of Telford' as a result of its pristine condition and quiet running. Following its renovation, instructions were given that only basic maintenance to ensure safe operation was to be carried out in the future on the type as the tramway conversion policy was reconfirmed. As Leeds No 526, No 2085 was to survive through to the system's final conversion in November 1959; subsequently preserved, the tram is now part of the Seashore Trolley Museum collection in the USA. (F.N.T. Lloyd-Jones/Online Transport Archive)

86 • THE LONDON FELTHAM TRAM

As an ex-Leyton UDC 'E/3' heads eastbound on 24 March 1951 with a route 62 service from Forest Hill to Savoy Street, No 2127 travels west along the Embankment with a service towards Croydon and Purley. (Julian Thompson/Online Transport Archive)

With Streatham Library in the background, No 2160 heads southbound on 25 March 1951 with a service towards Croydon and Purley. Streatham Library was opened in 1890; it was backed by Henry Tate – famous as the sugar magnate who founded the future Tate Gallery – who employed Sidney Smith, who also designed the Tate Gallery, as architect. No 2160 was ex-LUT No 391; it was to become Leeds Corporation No 583 in 1952. It remained in service until March 1957 and was scrapped six months later. (Julian Thompson/Online Transport Archive)

LAST YEARS IN LONDON • 87

Pictured at County Hall on 1 April 1951 is No 2129; routes 16 and 18 – from the Embankment to Croydon and Purley – were to be converted to bus operation on 7/8 April 1951 as part of Stage 3 of 'Operation Tramaway'. All the surviving 'Felthams' were withdrawn from service following this conversion. Route 16 operated clockwise from Kennington via the Embankment, Blackfriars and Elephant & Castle to Kennington; route 18 operated anti-clockwise. (Julian Thompson/Online Transport Archive)

Standing amongst scrap controllers removed from dismantled trams and withdrawn cars awaiting their fate, No 2079 was finally withdrawn in April 1951. Unlike the trams in the background, No 2079 was to escape Penhall Road and see further service. As Leeds No 550, it re-entered service in September 1951 and was to survive through until September 1957. (Harry Luff/Online Transport Archive)

88 • THE LONDON FELTHAM TRAM

A withdrawn 'Feltham' stands in the 'Tramatorium' at Penhall Road; unlike the vast majority of withdrawn trams that ended up awaiting their fate at Penhall Road, most of the 'Felthams' were to be sent north to Leeds for a further period of service. Access to the numerous sidings on which the withdrawn trams stood awaiting their ultimate fate was provided via an electrically-powered traverser. (W. J. Wyse/LRTA (London Area) Collection/Online Transport Archive)

Ex-LUT No 2138 was one of the numerous 'Felthams' withdrawn in April 1951 and is pictured here on a low-loader making its final journey in London en route to Leeds. It was to re-enter service later the same year as Leeds No 554; exchanging fleet numbers with No 517 in February 1959, the car was the only ex-LUT 'Feltham' to survive through to the system's closure (although it had been withdrawn in May 1959). Preserved following the system's abandonment, it was transferred to the Middleton Railway on 26 March 1961. Unfortunately, along with other trams stored there, the 'Feltham' suffered serious damage from vandalism and was subsequently scrapped; its bogies were, however, to survive and can now be found under the restored 'E/1' No 1622 at Crich. (J. Joyce Collection/Online Transport Archive)

The last 'Feltham' to be transferred north to Leeds was No 2158, which made its journey to Yorkshire on 3 October 1951. It is seen here at Penhall Road shortly before this move. It was to become Leeds No 590 when it re-entered service the following year. (Phil Tatt/Online Transport Archive)

Those withdrawn at this stage were Nos 2068/79/89/90/92/94/95/98/101/104/106/107/110-112/114/117/119. The remaining 'Felthams' were allocated to routes 16 and 18. No 2079 was – uniquely – to be retrieved from Penhall Road for a final swansong in London when it was used on an enthusiasts' tour on 7 April 1951 – the first day of the Stage 3 changeover – when, amongst other sections of line traversed, it operated over the track along Lambeth Palace Road and Albert Embankment that had been retained for possible diversionary use following Stage 2 of 'Operation Tramaway' in January. A further withdrawal occurred prior to the next stage of 'Operation Tramaway' when early in 1951, No 2139 was damaged in an accident; again repaired, it was sent to Leeds in March 1951, becoming No 551, where it was the first of the ex-LUT 'Felthams' to enter service in October the same year.

The operation of 'Felthams' in London came to an end with Stage 3 of 'Operation Tramaway' on 7/8 April 1951 when routes 16, 18 and 42 were converted. This resulted in all the surviving ex-LUT cars – Nos 2120/121/123-129/131-138/140-143/145-161/164 – being transferred to Penhall Road pending movement to Leeds. On 11 July 1951 the following were noted remaining in Penhall Road awaiting transfer: Nos 2142/143/145-147/153/157-159. This process was completed on 3 October 1951 when No 2158 departed from Penhall Road en route to the West Riding.

SUNDERLAND

With the conversion of the ex-MET routes and the consequent reduction in the tram fleet, No 2168 – although still relatively new – was deemed surplus to requirements as a result of its non-standard control gear and unique bogies. Another factor in the decision was that the transfer of the 'Felthams' to the south London routes meant that they required fitting with equipment to accommodate the conduit plough. The production 'Felthams', with doors adjacent to the platforms, were suitable for this treatment; No 331's central doors made this impractical and so the car was limited to those routes that were fitted with overhead throughout. As a result, No 2168 was withdrawn in August 1936.

During the 1930s, Sunderland Corporation supplemented its fleet through the purchase of a number of second-hand trams. The first of these to arrive was Portsmouth No 1, which was acquired by Sunderland in 1936, and this was followed by LPTB No 2168, which was purchased for £250 and delivered in March 1937. The cost of the tram's transport to Wearside added a further £548 to the purchase price.

Prior to the tram entering service in Sunderland, a number of modifications were made. The two trolleypoles were replaced by a centrally located

With the familiar profile of the River Wear bridge in the background, Sunderland No 100 – ex-MET No 331 and LPTB No 2168 – stands in Fawcett Street in August 1947. (Ian L. Wright/Online Transport Archive)

With a service heading for Durham Road from Seaburn, Sunderland No 100 is pictured heading southbound on Fulwell Lane as it approaches the level crossing with the freight-only branch that headed to the docks on the north side of the River Wear. (J. Joyce Collection/Online Transport Archive)

pantograph, whilst the automatic control of the doors was removed as were the driver's seats in the cabs. In addition the four 35hp motors – making it the most powerful tram to operate in Sunderland – and gearing were altered slightly to cater for the gradients on the Sunderland system. In service, No 100 – as the tram was renumbered – was to be found primarily on the Durham Road route.

The outbreak of war in September 1939 resulted in the temporary suspension of the route from Roker via Whitburn Road to Sea Lane – from 5 December 1939 – and traffic, particularly the holiday crowds that used to flock to the coast, was much reduced. As a result, a number of trams – including No 100 – were placed in store for much of the war.

In January 1947, Sunderland Corporation decided to replace its trams with buses. The process of conversion commenced in November 1950 and, from early 1951, the process of reducing the tram fleet commenced. Amongst the early casualties were the ex-Portsmouth tram – Sunderland No 99 – and No 100. These two trams were offered for sale and, whilst no other tramway was interested in either, No 100 was secured for preservation by the Light Railway Transport League – out of whose Museum Committee the Tramway Museum Society was eventually to emerge – under the auspices of the league's founder J.W. Fowler. The cost to acquire the tram was £100 but the most significant problem – in an era before the site at Crich was acquired – was storage.

Recorded on Holmeside on 28 May 1950, No 100 appears in reasonable external condition as it awaits its next duty. (F.K. Farrell/Online Transport Archive)

Standing in front of Hylton Road depot are the highest numbered trams in the Sunderland fleet. Behind No 100 is No 99; this was built by English Electric in 1934 and equipped with the same manufacturer's equal-wheel bogies. Entering service in 1934, the streamlined No 99 was stored during the Second World War, before being returned to service in 1946 having been repainted in the pre-war – and thus out-of-date – livery. No 99 was withdrawn in May 1951 and offered for sale in February the following year. Unfortunately, there was no one interested and the tram was sold for scrap in March 1953. (Phil Tatt/Online Transport Archive)

Pictured towards the end of its life on Wearside, No 100 is pictured on Durham Road. Stored during the war, No 100 was to be withdrawn in May 1951 and sold to the LRTL the following year. It was to remain in Sunderland until 1954, when it was moved to storage in Bishop Auckland; from there it went to Thornbury Works in Bradford before finally arriving at Crich during the summer of 1961. (R.W.A. Jones/Online Transport Archive)

OPERATION IN LEEDS

Of all the British tramway systems that survived after the Second World War, Leeds was considered to be one of the most secure; although there had been some retrenchment prior to 1939, these had affected mainly services beyond the city boundaries and had been offset by new routes and the purchase of new trams. During the war, the fleet had been increased by the purchase of second-hand trams from Hull and Sunderland, after the war, the corporation purchased further second-hand trams from Manchester and Southampton. Between 1946 and 1949, a number of short sections were again abandoned but these losses were offset by the opening – in two stages – of the Middleton circle connecting the existing Middleton and Belle Isle termini. The corporation also had long-term plans for the construction of tram subways under central Leeds and three experimental single-deckers – Nos 600-02 – were constructed in the early 1950s as a result.

Prior to and during the Second World War, the corporation had already acquired three ex-London Transport trams; these were Leeds Nos 277-79 and were 'HR/2' type cars rendered surplus to requirements in London following the conversion of route 11 – Highgate Village to Moorgate – to trolleybus operation on 10 December 1939. The three trams – ex-LT Nos 1881/83/86 respectively – travelled north to Leeds in August 1939, October 1939 and November 1939. The 'Felthams' – ideal for operation over reserved track sections (of which Leeds had a significant mileage) – attracted the interests of Leeds once London Transport had announced the renewed conversion programme.

Ex-LPTB No 2099 departed from the Metropolis at the end of September 1949 and, following a repaint in LT livery at Kirkstall Works but with Leeds Corporation insignia on its sides, the 'Feltham' entered service on 17 December 1949. Tested on a number of routes, the 'Feltham' generally performed well and It was decided to purchase the remaining cars as they were withdrawn by LT. (J. Joyce Collection/Online Transport Archive)

Having made the journey north, No 2099 reached Leeds on 1 October 1949; it is seen here the following day in Kirkstall Works awaiting unloading from the low loader that had transported it. (R.B. Parr/National Tramway Museum)

After its entry into service on 17 December 1949, No 2099 was tested on a number of routes. It is seen here at Crossgates departing with a trial run on route 16 to New Inn. (Barry Cross Collection/Online Transport Archive)

Pictured on 2 April 1950 on an enthusiasts' special, No 2099 stands in Middleton Woods whilst photographers record the occasion. The tour started at 10.30am with the Roundhay and Middleton circles being covered during the afternoon. The report in *Modern Tramway* recorded the fact that the tram – being then the only car in this livery – had been nicknamed by locals 'the red car'. (J. Joyce/Online Transport Archive)

The first of the Leeds 'Felthams' is pictured on the spur at Chapeltown on 2 April 1950; this was another location visited during the enthusiasts' tour held that day. This useful terminal stub – located at Stainbeck Lane – was a relatively late addition to the Leeds system, opening on 19 May 1948. (Barry Cross Collection/Online Transport Archive)

98 • THE LONDON FELTHAM TRAM

On 7 May 1950 No 2099 is pictured at Low Fields Road. The 'Feltham' was longer than most of Leeds' existing fleet; however, trackwork had already been modified in a number of places to accommodate the possible use of 44ft 0in long single-deck cars and this, allied to other work, allowed for the operation of the 'Felthams'. (Barry Cross Collection/Online Transport Archive)

No 2099 was not to retain its London number for long; renumbered 501 in August 1950 it is pictured here in September 1950 although still retaining the LT livery into which it had been repainted before entering service in Leeds. (Geoffrey Ashwell/Online Transport Archive)

Following the successful operation of No 2099, the next 'Feltham' to head to Leeds was No 2097, which arrived in Yorkshire on 12 August 1950. Exactly one month later it was to emerge as No 502 in an experimental livery of primarily red and white but with green window surrounds. Having formally entered service on 22 September 1950, it ran with this version of the livery for a short period before the green window surrounds were replaced by red. It is pictured here in the short-lived revised experimental livery with red window surrounds. No 502 was to survive in service until March 1959. (Phil Tatt/Online Transport Archive)

No 502 is pictured again, this time on an enthusiasts' special on 8 October 1950, heading northbound towards the city, having just passed under the railway bridge that carried the ex-LNER line from Beeston Junction to Hunslet over the Middleton tram route. (Barry Cross Collection/Online Transport Archive)

When No 503 entered service on 25 August 1950, it sported a further livery variation – all-over red. It is seen in this livery at the terminus of the Dewsbury Road service. (W.J. Wyse/LRTA (London Area) Collection/Online Transport Archive)

Following negotiations, No 2099 was sent northwards on an experimental basis; it reached Leeds on 1 October 1949 but before entering service some work was undertaken on it. The interior woodwork was polished although the original London Transport brown moquette was retained; externally, it was repainted in LT livery, albeit with Leeds Corporation insignia whilst retaining its original LT fleet number. Following a number of test runs during November 1949 and a day on display in City Square, No 2099 entered service in Leeds on 17 December 1949 and saw service on a number of routes during December 1949 and January, including Bramley and the Roundhay and Middleton circles. Although operation was not without its problems – hunting, for example, at high speed was noted – the new car drew generally favourable comments. According to a report in *Modern Tramway* in January 1950, 'The comments of passengers and passers-by are gratifying – approval seems universal, and people are eagerly awaiting the day when the routes they use are exclusively operated by cars of this type.'

On 20 February 1950, following the appointment of Albert Black Findlay from Glasgow as the new general manager (in place of William Vane Morland, who had held the position since April 1932), the transport committee agreed the purchase of ninety-two trams at £500 each. The purchase eventually comprised the ninety surviving 'Felthams', following the loss of Nos 2144/62, and the unique No 1.

When No 506 – ex-LPTB No 2066 – entered service on 6 November 1950, it wore the version of the red livery with two white bands between the windows and white band on the front dashes below the windscreen that was effectively to become the standard livery for the 'Felthams' during their operation in Leeds. The fleet numbers, in Gill Sans, were initially in gilt but, due to problems with visibility, these were replaced by Prussian blue initially and later black numerals. The transfer of a number of 'Felthams' to Swinegate in mid-1951 saw the type operate over a wider range of routes, including route 4 to Kirkstall Abbey. (Barry Cross Collection/Online Transport Archive)

No 507 – ex-LPTB No 2070 – entered service in Leeds on 14 November 1950; it is seen here alongside 'Horsfield' No 204. The 'Feltham' is seen here in the non-standard livery – of BET red with narrow white bands below the windows on both decks and a broader white band above the lower-deck windows – that was carried by only Nos 502, 504, 505 and 507; No 507 was, however, was destined to have a short second career. (Barry Cross Collection/Online Transport Archive)

On Sunday, 3 June 1951, No 509 was used by the LRTL for a tour of the Leeds system and is seen at Half Mile Lane on route 14. It operated from delivery to Leeds in a non-standard livery. It had been repainted in London shortly before despatch northwards and retained its London livery save for the addition of cream bands below the driver's cab windows, the lining out and the repainting of the centre two side panels on each side – in the slightly darker Leeds red – in order to accommodate the corporation crest. No 509 was subsequently repainted into standard Leeds red and cream. (J. Joyce/Online Transport Archive)

With the purchase agreed, the process of transferring the trams commenced on 12 August 1950 when No 2097 (Leeds No 502) reached the West Riding. The process of moving the cars northwards continued for just over a year with the last – LT No 2158 (Leeds No 590) – arriving in the city on 6 October 1951. For the movement north, bodies and bogies were separated; the former travelled fixed to a trailer whilst the latter were carried on a flat-bed section of the tractor unit. As a result, most of the 'Felthams' re-entered service in Leeds on bogies that had originally been used under other trams; the only exceptions were Nos 2082 and 2100 that retained their original bogies. No 2099 initially operated with its original bogies, but these were replaced by those from No 2074 (Leeds No 510) in June 1951. No 2099 operated with its LT number until it was renumbered 501 on 3 August 1950. Leeds had adopted a system of classifying its trams; the ex-MET cars became Class UCC/1 whilst the ex-LUT examples became 'UCC/2'.

On arrival in Leeds, each of the trams was taken to Kirkstall Works where work was undertaken to make them fit for service. The bodies were generally found to be sound – although there was the inevitable damage to panels that required repairing – but work was undertaken on the bogies, including the removal of the plough gear and the reprofiling of the wheels.

No 509 is seen again on the 1951 LRTL tour this time with the Pavilion Cinema as the backdrop as it makes its way westbound towards the terminus at Stanningley. The service to Stanningley was destined to be a relatively early casualty following the change of political power in May 1953 when the anti-tram Labour council took charge. The route was converted to bus operation on 3 October 1953. The Pavilion Cinema opened originally in late February 1920 and was to survive until final closure in April 1970; the building – albeit modified – still survives and has been converted into office accommodation. (Roy Brook/National Tramway Museum)

When the 'Felthams' first entered service in Leeds, they were allocated to Torre Road depot. No 516 – ex-MET No 336 and LPTB No 2080 – is seen here outside the depot on the single track up Torre Road that accessed it. No 516 entered service in Leeds on 18 January 1951 and was to be withdrawn in early 1957. Torre Road depot was originally opened on 4 April 1937 to accommodate both buses and trams; it was to lose its allocation of the latter on 19 November 1955. Finally closed as a bus depot in 1996, it was subsequently demolished. (Harry Luff/Online Transport Archive)

In January 1951, No 517 – ex-MET 378 and LPTB No 2118 – entered service fitted with a pantograph. In March and April, a further three cars – Nos 528-30 – also entered service fitted with pantographs; the use of the pantographs was, however, short-lived and all four cars received bow collectors by June 1951. No 517 is pictured whilst fitted with a pantograph with a route 15 service to Whingate at Crossgates. (J. Joyce Collection/Online Transport Archive)

Pictured on 24 March 1951 – a week before it entered service – No 530 looks in fine external condition and sports the pantograph that it was fitted with when it first operated in Leeds. (Barry Cross Collection/Online Transport Archive)

OPERATION IN LEEDS • 105

When it first entered service in Leeds on 3 October 1950, No 503 appeared in a lined-out all-red livery with black roof as shown in this view taken in May 1951 of it heading west with a service towards Whingate. Victor J. Matterface, the corporation's Tramways Rolling Stock Engineer, was appointed to the position in March 1948; he had previously been employed by the LTE and it was on his recommendation that Leeds pursued the purchase of the 'Feltham' cars following their withdrawal in London. He was also instrumental in seeing the Leeds tram fleet adopt a predominantly red livery. (W.J. Wyse/LRTA (London Area) Collection/Online Transport Archive)

Heading eastbound out of the city centre with a service towards Crossgates is No 524. This car had re-entered service on 28 February 1951. Whilst the majority of the 'Felthams' in Leeds had red paint – either BET or Post Office – supplied by Kearsley's, No 524 was one of four – the others being Nos 517, 526 and 528 – where the red paint was supplied by an alternative manufacturer. (Frank Hunt/LRTA (London Area) Collection/Online Transport Archive)

106 • THE LONDON FELTHAM TRAM

It's early 1951 and work on No 531 approaches its conclusion in Kirkstall Works. The tram was destined to enter service in Leeds on 21 April 1951. On the right is No 538 – note the chalked fleet numbers on the underframes of both trams – which was to make its debut on 28 May 1951. No 538 had originally been MET No 350 and LPTB No 2094. Both of these trams remained in service until the final day of operation in Leeds; indeed, No 531 was destined to operate the last service tram from Temple Newsam on that fateful day. (R.B. Parr/National Tramway Museum)

The small side destination boxes at the front of the trams were not required and these were painted over. In Leeds, the cars operated using a single destination blind that incorporated both the route number and destination. The trams were also fitted with bow collectors in place of their existing trolleypoles. Internally, damaged seats were repaired and all the woodwork was re-varnished.

Prior to the arrival of the 'Felthams', the standard tram livery in Leeds had been blue. However, Vic Matterface, the corporation's rolling stock engineer, who had been instrumental in acquiring the 'Felthams', was keen to see the blue, which he believed faded badly, replaced by red. Following the arrival of No 2099 and its repainting in red at Kirkstall, allied to Matterface's persuasion of Councillor John Rafferty (chairman of the transport committee), it was agreed on 15 May 1950 that, for the future, the buses would be painted green and the trams red. The early 'Feltham' cars in Leeds were to sport a variety of experimental liveries before a final one was determined.

No 502 emerged in September 1950 with a predominantly red livery but with green window surrounds; this was short-lived and the green was soon replaced by red. It was to undergo a further modification by early October with two white bands being added between the upper and lower deck windows. No 503 was to emerge later in September with an all-over red livery whilst Nos 504 and 505 appeared the following month in the modified livery now carried by No 502. No 506 entered service in November 1950 with a further modification; this was the addition of a white band beneath the windscreen on

No 539, which entered service in Leeds on 17 May 1951, is seen heading westbound through City Square with a service towards New Inn when relatively new. In the distance can be seen one of Bradford Corporation's batch of 'tin front' AEC Regent IIIs with East Lancs bodies (Nos 66-105) on the joint service linking the two cities. Behind the tram can be seen the Majestic Cinema. Designed by Pascal J. Steinlet and Joseph C. Maxwell, the cinema was situated on the corner of Wellington Street and Quebec Street and opened on 5 June 1922. It closed as a cinema in 1969, being used for bingo until 1996. The listed but vacant – although converted – building was to suffer serious fire damage in September 2014. (Frank Hunt/LRTA (London Area) Collection/Online Transport Archive)

No 531 – originally MET No 362 and LPTB No 2106 – was one of a number of 'Felthams' that entered service in January 1951. It is recorded here at the Crossgates terminus of route 15 with a cross-city service to Whingate when virtually newly out of Kirkstall Works. The service to Whingate was only renumbered as route 15 on 1 October 1950. (Phil Tatt/Online Transport Archive)

Following withdrawal in London during April 1951, No 2157 was transferred to Leeds where it is seen – still in its original London Transport condition – in Kirkstall Works. It would emerge during 1952 as Leeds No 586. It survived in service until September 1957.
(Geoffrey Ashwell/Online Transport Archive)

When No 509 entered service on 3 October 1950, it did so in a non-standard livery with only the central panels on both sides repainted into Leeds red. It is seen here in August 1952 still sporting the unique livery as it awaits departure with a service to Gipton. (W.J. Wyse/LRTA (London Area) Collection/Online Transport Archive)

No 535 – which had entered service in Leeds on 1 May 1951 – is pictured at Crossgates bound for New Inn on 1 May 1951. (R.L. Wilson/Online Transport Archive)

On 4 September 1952, No 507 was involved in a spectacular accident when it ran away from the Roundhay Park terminus and ran into the back of No 92 at Oakwood, seriously damaging both trams. Fortunately, there were no fatalities, although the driver of No 92 was knocked unconscious. No 92 was condemned immediately but No 507 – seen here at rest having derailed – was retained unrepaired until it was scrapped on 24 August 1955. (R.F. Mack)

No 548 entered service in Leeds on 24 August 1951 and is seen here a year later – on 8 September 1952 – heading outbound up York Road with a route 15 service to Whingate. (John Meredith/Online Transport Archive)

OPERATION IN LEEDS • 111

On 13 May 1953, 'Feltham' No 558 is seen alongside two of the single-deck trams – Nos 601 and 602 – that had not yet entered passenger service. Nos 601 and 602 were both fitted with bodies supplied by the local bodybuilder Charles H. Roe Ltd and were painted in a non-standard purple and white livery to mark the coronation of HM Queen Elizabeth II. They are seen here on the second of a two-day Ministry of Transport inspection undertaken by Brigadier C.A. Langley. No 558 had originally been LUT No 351 and LPTB No 2121. Following its original withdrawal in April 1951, it re-entered service in Leeds on 12 December 1951. Its career in the West Riding was to last until withdrawal in September 1957 and scrapping at Low Fields Road the following month. (R.B. Parr/National Tramway Museum)

each dash. This was to become the standard livery for the future although minor variations continued. No 509 appeared in December 1950 with white window surround but no upper white band below the upper-deck windows. The predominant red was a shade similar to that used on BET buses but three – Nos 525/31/38 – emerged in a lighter shade of red. From June 1953, when cars were repainted, the straw lining out was omitted and a number of the ex-LUT 'Felthams' entered service in this modified form.

The work of repainting the 'Felthams' required a slight modification of the track at Kirkstall Works. As the paint shop could only be accessed via the traverser – for which the 'Felthams' were too long – a new line was laid to enable the trams to reach the paint shop without the need to use the traverser.

The operation of the 'Felthams' in Leeds was facilitated by a post-war policy, undertaken in connection with the possible subway scheme, of realigning junctions to permit the operation of 44ft 0in long single-deck bogie cars. The anticipated arrival of ninety 'Felthams' resulted in more work being undertaken. When first in service in Leeds, No 2099 was allocated to Torre Road depot; this provided cars for the cross-city services linking Cross Gates, Halton, New Inn and Whingate plus Temple Newsam.

During the summer of 1953 Britain celebrated the coronation of HM Queen Elizabeth II and, on 9 June (exactly a week after the event), No 511 is seen in City Square amidst the celebratory decorations. No 511 – ex-MET No 361 and LPTB No 2105 – entered service in Leeds on 19 January 1951 but was destined to be a relatively early casualty, being withdrawn in early August 1957 and being scrapped two months later. (R.B. Parr/National Tramway Museum)

On 31 July 1953, No 516 is seen as passengers board at the Corn Exchange terminus of route 10 to Compton Road. The section of track on which No 516 is pictured was modified during the Second World War, with work being completed on its doubling during 1942, and was further improved during early 1953 when it was tripled for much of its length with the completion of the long loop outside the Corn Exchange to serve the loading barriers. The Compton Road route was to be converted to bus operation on 3 April 1954. No 516 was originally MET No 336 and LPTB No 2080; withdrawn originally in September 1950, it re-entered service in Leeds on 18 January 1951. Never fitted with one-piece windscreens, No 516 was – in March 1957 – one of the first of the ex-MET 'Felthams' to be withdrawn in Leeds and was to be scrapped six months later at Low Fields Road. (R.B. Parr/National tramway Museum)

On 7 August 1954 No 536 stands in City Square with an eastbound service on route 18 towards Crossgates. If the corporation's ambitious plans for a network of tram subways under the city had been completed, trams would have accessed City Square below street level. (R.L. Wilson/Online Transport Archive)

Heading westbound at Halton Dial through the snow on 18 January 1955 is No 545 with a service from Crossgates to Whingate. The routes heading to the south are those to Temple Newsam and Halton. (R.B. Parr/National Tramway Museum)

114 • THE LONDON FELTHAM TRAM

A line-up of 'Felthams' still in London livery await attention alongside 1928-built No 407. This was one of the Leeds trams fitted with EMB Pivotal four-wheel trucks and was one of five delivered in 1928. Whilst one was to receive a replacement Peckham P35 truck, the unmodified quartet – including No 407 – were all withdrawn during 1951 and 1952. 'Feltham' No 2141 – ex-LUT No 372 – was to become Leeds No 570, entering service in October 1955. It was destined to have a short second career, being withdrawn in September 1957. (J. Joyce Collection/Online Transport Archive)

Initially all of the early 'Felthams' were based at Torre Road but, in June 1951, two – Nos 504 and 505 – were transferred to Swinegate and introduced to services to Moortown via Harehills (route 3), Kirkstall Abbey (route 4), Dewsbury Road (route 9), Compton (route 10) and Gipton (route 11). By mid-1952, some 20 'Felthams' – Nos 501-20 – were all operating from Swinegate.

On 18 February 1951, No 517 appeared sporting an ex-Sunderland pantograph rather than its bow collector. The experimental use of pantographs was extended in March and April when Nos 528-30 entered service with them. However, an accident on 18 May 1951 – when No 517 brought down the overhead at the junction of Wellington Street and City Square – resulted in the end of the use of pantographs. The incident caused the pantograph to be catapulted on to the roof of the adjacent Majestic cinema. The primary cause of the incident was that the pantograph – being centrally mounted – could not cope with overhead aligned to permit the operation of the rear-facing bow collectors.

Whilst a number of the ex-LUT 'Felthams' entered service during 1955 and 1956, a number – including ex-LPTB No 2135 (which was scheduled to become Leeds No 584) – remained out of use. These cars were to be scrapped without further service and two of the unused 'Felthams' are seen awaiting their fate in the yard at Low Fields Road in late 1956. (Barry Cross Collection/Online Transport Archive)

The Dewsbury Road route was one of two services converted to bus operation on 28 September 1957. Pictured here heading outbound is No 514; this had originally been MET No 371 and LT No 2115. (F.E.J. Ward/Online Transport Archive)

On 21 July 1956, Nos 502 and 510 are pictured at Whingate, the western terminus of the cross-city service to Crossgates. The 17 was a short working of that service that terminated at Harehills Lane and it was unusual to see two cars on the short working at Whingate at the same time. No 502 was ex-LPTB No 2097 and No 510 was ex-LPTB No 2074. They had entered service in Leeds on 3 October 1950 and 22 November 1950 respectively. The latter was one of a handful of the type taken out of service during 1958 but not scrapped until July 1959 – in the yard of George Cohen & Sons Ltd in Holbeck – whilst No 502 was to survive until March 1959. It was also scrapped in July 1959, this time at Low Fields Road. (R.B. Parr/National Tramway Museum)

Pictured heading outbound on the private right of way from Moor Road towards Middleton Park Road is No 574. The tram is about to pass over the level crossing with the branch off the historic Middleton Railway. No 574 – previously LUT No 360 and LPTB No 2129 – was the penultimate 'Feltham' to enter service in Leeds – on 5 July 1956 – with the last being No 582 later the same month. Prior to re-entering service, No 574 had been modified by the incorporation of one-piece windscreens and replacement MVOK9B controllers. It was destined to have a relatively short second career, being withdrawn in March 1959 and being scrapped at the Brown Lane, Holbeck, works of George Cohen & Sons Ltd six months later. (D.W.K. Jones Collection/Online Transport Archive)

Another service to survive to the end was route 20 to Halton. Recorded passing through City Square en route to York Road and its ultimate destination is No 531; this was originally MET No 362 and later LT No 2106. It was one of the 'Feltham' cars that survived through until the final abandonment of the Leeds system.
(R.W.A. Jones/Online Transport Archive)

Leeds operated a number of cross-city routes and route 20 operated from Halton through to New Inn until the New Inn and Whingate routes were converted to bus operation on 21 July 1956. No 532, seen here at the New Inn terminus, was originally MET No 352 and later LPTB No 2096. This was another of the trams that survived through until November 1959.
(R.W.A. Jones/Online Transport Archive)

Seen emerging during April 1954 from the single-track section along Kirkgate that brought city-bound trams in from the York Road corridor and other routes to the east of the city centre is No 526 with a cross-city service to Whingate. Outbound cars operated along the single track along New York Street, to the left of the Yorkshire Penny Bank, and York Street. No 526 had been new as MET No 341 and then LPTB No 2085; withdrawn in September 1950 it entered service in Leeds in 1951. Surviving through to final closure in November 1959, No 526 was one of two of the ex-MET cars to be preserved. It is currently based – in a poor condition – at the Seashore Trolley Museum at Kennebunkport in the USA. (Phil Tatt/Online Transport Archive)

No-one was – fortunately – injured but the quartet of pantograph-fitted cars were refitted with bow collectors the following month. During the summer of 1952 it was reported that No 519 was in Kirkstall Works pending conversion into a single-deck car; this was not proceeded with, however, as the integral design of the bodywork precluded the conversion.

By this date, a total of sixty-eight of the 'Felthams' – all of the ex-MET cars and eighteen of the ex-LUT vehicles – had entered service. However, the work involved at Kirkstall in making the trams ready for service had resulted in reduced maintenance work on the remainder of the fleet and, with the introduction of No 590 on 27 May 1952, work largely ceased on the type; prior to this date, Nos 563-66/70/80/89 had received some attention to their interiors and were repainted externally, although none were to enter service at this time. The staff at Kirkstall Road soon discovered that the ex-LUT cars were in poor condition when compared to the ex-MET batch and that the GEC contactor equipment was less reliable.

No 531 is pictured again, this time emerging from Swinegate depot into Swinegate itself during April 1954. The depot was originally opened on 13 October 1914 but its immediate use by tramcars was limited as it was soon requisitioned by the military for use in the First World War. After the war, the depot was significantly enlarged, with work being completed in May 1931. As extended, the depot provided accommodation for almost 200 trams. As the tram network declined, Swinegate was to become the last operational depot and, from November 1957 when work ceased on trams at Kirkstall Road Works, was adapted to undertake limited maintenance work, including repainting, on the surviving trams. The track on the left led to the Permanent Way Yard whilst those in the foreground were used by service cars. (Phil Tatt/Online Transport Archive)

Leeds No 523 recorded at the terminus of route 22 at Temple Newsam. This had originally been MET No 352 and LPTB No 2096 prior to withdrawal in September 1950; re-entering service in September 1951, the tram was to survive through until the closure of the Leeds system in November 1959. The track on the right with the buffer stop had allowed trams to be stabled at this terminus as a wartime measure during the Second World War. (Phil Tatt/Online Transport Archive)

The services from the city centre westwards to Whingate and New Inn were converted to bus operation on 21 July 1956. Pictured at the latter terminus during April 1954 is No 549 with a cross-city service to Halton. This tram – originally MET No 373 and LPTB No 2117 – was withdrawn in January 1951 and entered service in Leeds later the same year. It was withdrawn for the second time in March 1959. (Phil Tatt/Online Transport Archive)

OPERATION IN LEEDS • 121

With the impressive façade of Leeds City station, as rebuilt during the 1930s with the Queen's Hotel, on the left and the Majestic Cinema in the background, No 543 is seen during April 1954 in Wellington Street, on the south side of City Square, as a passenger disembarks. The tram will then head into Boar Lane en route to Halton. No 543 was originally MET No 351 and LPTB No 2095. Withdrawn in London in January 1951, it was to re-enter service in Leeds on 20 June 1951. It was to survive almost six years in the West Riding before withdrawal in April 1957 and scrapping at Low Field Road four months later. (Phil Tatt/Online Transport Archive)

The first withdrawal of a 'Feltham' in Leeds occurred following an incident involving No 507. On 4 September 1952, the tram was being reversed at the Roundhay Park terminus. With the driver temporarily absent, the car started to run away and, with the conductor having failed to stop the car using either the hand parking brake or the emergency air brake (the subsequent Ministry of Transport enquiry revealed not only that the conductor was unaware of the location of the latter but also the training did not include physically showing them the location – it was situated just outside the driver's cab and painted red – but just referring to it), the car proceeded at an increasing speed towards Oakwood. No 507 was then to collide with 'Chamberlain' car No 92 before becoming derailed.

No 581 is seen at Whingate with a service to Crossgates during April 1954. This had originally been LUT No 374 and LPTB No 2143 before entering service in Leeds in January 1952. It was to survive in service until early January 1958 but was not finally scrapped until April 1959. (Phil Tatt/Online Transport Archive)

As 'Horsfield' No 190 heads southbound, No 527 is seen crossing City Square, prior to entering Boar Lane, with a service towards Crossgates. The 'Feltham' had originally been MET No 329 and LPTB No 2075; withdrawn in London during September 1950, the tram re-entered service in Leeds on 13 March 1951. In July 1957, No 527 exchanged numbers with No 528; this was followed – contemporaneously with its withdrawal – by a further exchange, this time with No 539, prior to being scrapped at Low Fields Road in October 1957. The new No 527 – ex-No 539 – was to survive until withdrawal in November 1959. Also visible in the background is a Bradford Corporation bus, on the joint service linking the two cities. The impressive building that forms the backdrop of this view is the old General Post Office; designed by Sir Henry Tanner, the building, which is now Grade II listed, was opened in 1896. (Phil Tatt/Online Transport Archive)

OPERATION IN LEEDS • 123

No 586 – one of the ex-LUT cars – is seen in Wellington Street during April 1955 with a cross-city service towards Crossgates. Entering services in Leeds during February 1952, the tram was to see just over five years' service in the West Riding. (Phil Tatt/Online Transport Archive)

Recorded at the terminus at Crossgates during April 1955 is No 529; this had originally been MET No 372 and LPTB No 2116 prior to being sold to Leeds Corporation. It entered service in the West Riding on 2 April 1951 and is pictured here prior to September 1955 when it received a one-piece windscreen. No 529 was one of the type that survived through to the final day of operation and was amongst the last to be scrapped, succumbing finally in February 1960. (Phil Tatt/Online Transport Archive)

Leeds No 565 stands at the Temple Newsam terminus during April 1955. No 565 had originally been LUT No 357 and LPTB No 2126 before entering service with Leeds Corporation in February 1955. It was one of seven of the ex-LUT cars that had been refurbished and repainted by Leeds but which had not entered service; all seven – Nos 563-66/70/80/89 – were made operational during February and March 1955. No 565 was to survive in service until March 1959. (Phil Tatt/Online Transport Archive)

OPERATION IN LEEDS

Leeds No 586 – ex-LUT No 388 and LPTB No 2157 – heads along Wellington Street during April 1955 with a Crossgates service. No 586 was withdrawn in September 1957. (Phil Tatt/Online Transport Archive)

Fortunately, there were no fatalities – the conductor of No 507 had jumped from the tram as it departed whilst the conductor of No 92 had issued a warning and he and a number of passengers on the rear platform of No 92 also managed to jump clear although the driver was injured – but both trams were seriously damaged. No 92 was withdrawn immediately although it was not until July 1953 that No 507 was formally withdrawn; it was scrapped two years later – the first 'Feltham' to be scrapped by the corporation. The enquiry was handled by Brigadier Langley and No 515 was used for test purposes. The report concluded that the primary fault lay with the driver of the 'Feltham', who had failed to apply the handbrake, but Langley recommended that the training of conductors be improved.

By the early 1950s, the position of the tram in Leeds was becoming a political issue. Traffic congestion was an increasing problem – particularly in the city centre – and led to revived thoughts about the possibility of subways (and to the construction of the three single-deck cars, Nos 600-02). There was also a deterioration in the finances of the transport department. The election of a new – Conservative-led – council in 1951 had resulted in a review of transport policy and the conversion of a short section of the route to Stanningley; there was, however, no serious threat to the survival of the tramway network at this time. The sea change came on 6 March 1953 when the local Labour Party adopted a policy of tramway conversion; when they won control of the council in May, the writing was on the wall as the announcement was made that the two biggest loss-making tram routes – to Stanningley and Kirkstall – were to be converted to bus operation. The former succumbed on 3 October 1953 and, a month later (on 3 November), it was announced that all the remaining tram routes were to be converted over a ten-year period.

Pictured at the Halton terminus is No 541; the service from the city centre to New Inn was converted to bus operation on 21 July 1956 but the route to Halton was to survive to become one of the last routes in Leeds, being finally converted on 7 November 1959. No 541 had originally been LPTB No 2107. Re-entering service in Leeds in 1951, it was to survive until October 1956 – one of the earliest to be withdrawn – although it was not to be scrapped until September 1957. (R.W.A. Jones/Online Transport Archive)

Leading the anti-tram faction was the chairman of the transport committee, Councillor Rafferty, whilst his Conservative opponent – Councillor Mather – was staunchly pro-tram. In this division, the council was replicating divisions within the transport department itself.

The conversion programme envisaged that, initially, it was to be the cross-city routes that would be handled first in order to alleviate congestion in the city centre; the routes with significant mileage of reserved track – such as those along York Road and via the Middleton circle – would be the last to be converted. These were the services for which the 'Felthams' were, in theory, ideally suited. Between 1954 and 1956, much of the reserved track on the York Road routes was re-laid. Due to the high axle weights of the 'Felthams', the condition of the track had deteriorated and this had severely affected the trams' axle springs and bolsters.

In late 1954, work commenced on getting a number of the remaining 'Felthams' ready for service. The first to emerge was No 563 in February 1955. This was modified before entering service; its original controllers were replaced by two interlocking MVOK9B units – probably re-used from withdrawn 'Pivotal' cars – in an attempt to reduce the type's tendency to slip on greasy track when starting on the

Heading eastbound along Boar Lane during April 1955 with a service towards Halton is No 528; the view was taken shortly before the tram was modified in July 1956 by the fitting of one-piece windscreens. No 528 had originally been MET No 342 and LPTB No 2086 prior to withdrawal in September 1950. Entering service in Leeds in March 1951 and it was to swop numbers with No 527 in late July 1957, shortly after it had been withdrawn. No 528 – or No 527 as it had become – was to be scrapped in September 1957. (Phil Tatt/Online Transport Archive)

city's many steep gradients. Also to enter service in February 1955 were Nos 565, 570 and 580. These were followed in March by Nos 564, 566 and 589; in April by No 567; in June by No 587; and in July by No 569. A further five entered service during 1956: No 568 in March; No 573 in April; No 585 in June; and Nos 574 and 582 in July. No 582 was the last tram to enter service in Leeds, on the 31st of the month. Of these trams, a further six, following on from No 563, were fitted with replacement MVOK9B controllers; these were Nos 568/73/74/82/85/87. By the date that No 582 entered service, Torre Road depot had closed – on 19 November 1955 – and all the operational 'Felthams' were now concentrated at Swinegate. One unplanned withdrawal occurred in late 1956 when, on 16 September, No 580 was involved in a collision near the railway bridge on Balm Road. The damaged tram was not repaired and was scrapped at Low Fields Road in July 1957.

Heading inbound on Tong Road from New Inn, Wortley, with a service to Halton is No 586. This location was the junction with the route to Whingate, which can be seen off heading to the right. Both sections were converted to bus operation on 21 July 1956; this led to a route reorganisation with the York Road routes 18 and 20 being interworked with the Middleton circle routes 12 and 26. No 586 was LPTB No 2157 and was transferred to Leeds following withdrawal in April 1951. Re-entering service the following year, it was to be withdrawn in September 1957. (R.W.A. Jones/Online Transport Archive)

In a programme that commenced in 1955, the majority of the type received one-piece windscreens. The first car to emerge with this modification was No 587 when it entered service in Leeds for the first time on 6 June 1955. The first of the ex-MET cars to be modified was No 509, which emerged on 11 August 1955. The last tram to receive the modification – and the only one so treated during 1957 (and more than a year after the penultimate example) – was No 519. All of the operational 'Felthams' were so modified with the exception of No 507 (which had already been withdrawn) and Nos 516/33/40/45/51/62.

No 545 heads inbound with a service towards New Inn as it turns from Kirkgate towards Duncan Street and Boar Lane. In the background can be seen the railway bridge that carries the main line from Leeds east towards York. No 545 was previously LPTB No 2111 and had re-entered service in Leeds during 1951. It was another car that survived until September 1957. (R.W.A. Jones/Online Transport Archive)

Leeds No 570, pictured here on the Roundhay service (route 3), was operational in Leeds for almost exactly two years. One of those cars that reached the West Riding in mid-1951 but then stored, the car only re-entered service in October 1955. Although the Roundhay service was to survive until 28 March 1959, No 570 had been withdrawn in October 1957. The tram shows to good effect the standard red livery adopted for use by the 'Felthams' in Leeds with the two white bands, the white stripes below the windscreens on the dash and the straw-coloured lining out on the panels. The fleet number on the front dash, in a Gill Sans typeface, is now in black; earlier, fleet numbers had appeared in gilt and then in Prussian blue. (Harry Luff/Online Transport Archive)

Recorded in Chapeltown, on the Roundhay loop, is Leeds No 583; this had originally been LUT No 391 (LPTB No 2160) and was one of a number of ex-LUT 'Felthams' to enter service in the West Riding during 1952. It was to survive in service until March 1957. No 583 carries the final simplified version of the standard red livery but without the straw lining out. A number of the ex-LUT cars – Nos 567-69/73/74/82/85/87 – entered service in this condition and when earlier cars were repainted after mid-1953 the distinctive lining out was omited on cost grounds. (Harry Luff/Online Transport Archive)

In September 1957, No 588 is emerging from Middleton Woods with a route 12 service bound for Middleton. The Middleton routes – which operated over the only post-war extension (the link from Belle Isle to Middleton that opened in two stages during 1949) – was to be converted to bus operation on 28 March 1959 but, by that date, No 588 had been withdrawn, although it was not to be scrapped until April 1959. (J. Joyce/Online Transport Archive)

OPERATION IN LEEDS • 131

Also recorded in September 1957, but this time at Temple Newsam, is No 504. This had originally been MET No 338 and LPTB No 2082 before withdrawal in August 1950. It was to re-enter service – as Leeds No 504 – two months later and was to survive through until towards the final closure of the system. (J. Joyce/Online Transport Archive)

One of the routes to survive through until the final closure of the Leeds system was that serving Crossgates; pictured at the terminus is No 538. The photograph post-dates November 1955 as the tram is fitted with the one-piece windscreen, which was fitted that month, and is shortly prior to the system's final closure as towards the end all service cars terminated at Corn Exchange. This tram – originally MET No 350 and LPTB No 2094 – was to enter service in Leeds during 1951. Surviving through until November 1959 and the system's demise, it was one of the few 'Feltham' cars to achieve some eight years of service. (J. Joyce/Online Transport Archive)

Recorded during 1959, No 532 descends from Temple Newsam with a service towards the Corn Exchange. This tram had originally been MET No 360 and LPTB No 2104, before re-entering service in Leeds on 7 April 1951. It was to survive through until the final closure of the system and was one of the last of the type to be scrapped towards the end of February 1960. The view shows to good effect the one-piece windscreen fitted to the majority of the operational 'Felthams'; No 532 was to receive this modification in early March 1956. (Phil Tatt/Online Transport Archive)

The fate of all bar three of the Leeds 'Felthams'; the body of No 568 – withdrawn prior to the final abandonment – is set on fire in the yard at Holbeck operated by George Cohen Ltd. The corporation policy of pulling the bodies over, so that they were burnt on their sides, dated to the early 1950s and concerns that, if the bodies were left upright when set alight, it was possible that somebody might be trapped on the upper deck. (Barry Cross Collection/Online Transport Archive)

In November 1958 No 524 – ex-MET No 332 and LPTB No 2076 – exchanged numbers with ex-LUT No 565. The ex-MET car is seen here being dismantled at Low Fields Road in April 1959; the ex-LUT car was to survive a further three months.
(Ian Stewart Collection/Online Transport Archive)

It's 3 October 1959 and the Leeds system has barely a month to survive before its final conversion as No 514 – ex-MET No 371 and LPTB No 2115 – heads past the Quarry Hill flats and the Central Bus Station with an inbound service on route 20 (although the blind shows 'Halton', often blinds were changed early on inbound journeys). Although Leeds retained the narrow front platform doors when the 'Felthams' entered service, these were not used for passengers but to permit the loading of prams and luggage as the notice adjacent to the door makes explicit. When upstairs, the conductors often made use of the sliding window to check that everyone had boarded before giving the driver the signal to proceed.
(R.L. Wilson/Online Transport Archive)

On 1 November 1959, less than a week before the system closed, the LRTL organised a tour of the remaining routes using No 501, the first of the 'Feltham' cars to arrive in the city, and 'Horsfield' No 189. The two cars are seen on the Lupton Avenue spur, off the main York Road route. Both trams were eventually to be preserved; No 501, as LT No 2099, is now part of the London Transport Museum collection whilst No 189 was acquired by the Tramway Museum Society and is now housed at the National Tramway Museum. (John Meredith/Online Transport Archive)

This work meant that seven 'Felthams' remained that had not entered service and these were all disposed of by the end of 1956. The first three – Nos 2151 (planned Leeds No 576), 2145 (planned Leeds No 577) and 2142 (planned Leeds No 578) – were scrapped at Kirkstall in July, August and September respectively. None of this trio had been renumbered and they retained their London livery to the end.

One factor in the decision to replace the controllers on most of the recent ex-LUT cars to enter service was the increasing problem of obtaining spares for the GEC equipped trams. This was not a problem alone for the ex-LUT 'Felthams' as the 'Horsfield' type was also adversely affected. July 1956 saw the withdrawal of the first operational 'Felthams' with the demise of three GEC-equipped cars – Nos 552/55/79 – which were all destined to be scrapped at Low Fields Road by the end of the year along with the final four trams that had not entered service these were ex-LT Nos 2155 (planned Leeds No 571); 2128 (planned Leeds No 572); 2156 (planned Leeds No 575); and 215 (planned Leeds No 584). These disposals meant that

Again recorded during the tour of 1 November 1959, No 501 is seen displaying a spurious route 26 destination at Halton Dial. The 26 – one of the services that had operated via the Middleton loop – had been converted to bus operation on 28 March 1959. The tour of Leeds had departed from Swinegate at about 10am and spent some three hours running over the surviving routes. The afternoon was to have been spent on a tour of the surviving Sheffield routes – as part of the LRTL's AGM weekend based in Bradford – but this had had to be cancelled as a result of strike action amongst the tram and bus crews in Sheffield. (F.K. Farrell/Online Transport Archive)

the Leeds fleet now comprised some seventy operational 'Felthams'; whilst the system was contracting, the majority of casualties at this time comprised older trams, such as the final 'Pivotal' cars. Although the end of the system was in sight, work continued on regular repaints at Kirkstall Works until November 1957. Other work undertaken on the type including modification to the sanding gear; this work, which was designed to prevent the trams running away on wet rails in Middleton Woods, allowed the type to appear regularly on the Middleton circular from July 1956.

In September 1957 there were two conversions – the services to Moortown via Chapeltown and to Dewsbury Road on the 28th of the month – and this resulted in the withdrawal of twenty-nine 'Felthams' between August and November 1957; these comprised eighteen BTH-fitted trams – Nos 503/05/08/11/16/27/28/30/33/37/40/41/43-45/47/48/50 – and eleven GEC cars – Nos 551/53/58-60/62/70/80/83/86/90. These were all scrapped at Low Fields Road by the end of the year. A twentieth BTH car – No 513 – was withdrawn in December 1957, following an electrical fire, but was not scrapped until April 1959. One feature of 'Feltham' operation during the last two years of the Leeds system was the

One final view of the tour held on 1 November 1959 illustrates the relatively poor condition externally of both of the trams used on the tour as the system approached the end. As the report in *Modern Tramway* noted: 'As the cars entered the city streets the sun broke through and sunshine accompanied the tour, helping to dispel the funereal atmosphere of this last occasion.' (W.J. Wyse/LRTA (London Area) Collection/Online Transport Archive)

renumbering of certain cars; full details of this can be found in the appendix.

The end of 1957 also witnessed the removal of the track connection to Kirkstall Works; thereafter, limited maintenance was undertaken at Swinegate with the trucks, if they required attention, being moved to and from Kirkstall by road. The depot at Swinegate also undertook any paintwork that was required and the paintwork on a number of trams – such as Nos 529/74/82 – received attention in early 1958. Although no routes were converted to bus operation during that year, the number of operational 'Felthams' was further reduced by the withdrawal of four ex-MET and 11 ex-LUT cars; none were scrapped during the year with the result that at the start of 1959 there were fifty 'Felthams' extant – thirty-one ex-MET and nineteen ex-LUT. All of the ex-LUT cars that remained in service were fitted with the OK9B controllers.

The first conversions of 1959 occurred on 28 March when three services – route 3 from Briggate to Moortown via Harehills, and the Middleton circle routes 12, 26 and 27 – were converted. This resulted in the sale of eleven trams for scrap; Joseph Standish Ltd of Hunslet acquired 522/54 (ex-517)/61 (ex-587)/81/88 whilst Johnson of Churwell took Nos 513/63/65 (ex-524)/66/67. These conversions were followed on 18 April by the replacement of trams by buses on route 25 from Swinegate to Hunslet.

OPERATION IN LEEDS • 137

The last day of tram operation in Leeds – Saturday, 7 November 1959 – saw twelve 'Felthams' in operation but the final procession comprised ten of the native 'Horsfield' cars. 'Feltham' No 531 was the last service car to depart from Temple Newsam at 4.37pm but the last of the type to operate in the city was No 512, seen here in the gloom of that final evening. Following its last evening duties, No 512 was scrapped at Swinegate on 17 February 1960 – one of the last of the non-preserved examples to survive. (C. Carter/Online Transport Archive)

Following this, George Cohen Ltd acquired 20 redundant 'Felthams' – Nos 502/09-11 (ex-519)/18/21/24 (ex-565)/35/36/49/56/57 (ex-564)/68/69/73/74/82/85/87 (ex-561)/89 – which were dismantled in a yard at Holbeck during June and July that year.

The closures of March and April resulted in the operational fleet of 'Felthams' being reduced to nineteen, of which only one – No 517 (ex-554) – was ex-LUT. Despite the imminence of closure, basic maintenance was still being undertaken; this included repair work to the bogies of No 526 during August (this work was one factor in the selection, eventually, of this car for preservation following the system's closure).

Of the nineteen surviving cars at closure, thirteen were to see service on the last day; these were Nos 501/05 (ex-520)/12/14/23/25/26/28 (ex-539)/29/31/32/38/42. The remaining six – Nos 504/06/15/17 (ex-554)/34/46 – were stored. The majority of the last services operated were handled by the surviving 'Horsfield' cars – as the final traditional Leeds trams in service – but No 531 was to be the last service car to Temple Newsam at 4.2pm whilst No 512 was to be the last 'Feltham' in public service later that evening.

Following the conversion of the final four services – route 17 to Harehills Lane, route 18 to Cross Gates, route 20 to Halton and route 22 to Temple Newsam – the remaining 'Feltham' cars – with the exception of the trio destined for preservation (Nos 501, 517 [ex-554] and 526) – were sold to J. W. Hinchcliffe Ltd and scrapped in Swinegate depot. The last survivors – Nos 504 and 520 – were dismantled in February 1960.

PRESERVATION

The are three 'Feltham' cars that survive in preservation: one of the prototypes and two of those supplied to MET.

Following its withdrawal in Sunderland in 1951, No 100 (originally MET No 331 and LPTB No 2168) was secured for preservation. After storage in a number of sites – including Bradford City Transport's Thornbury Works (where it was stored in close proximity to the then recently restored Bradford No 104) – the tram passed to the Tramway Museum at Crich, where it arrived in June 1961. A decade later the tram was cosmetically restored as MET No 331 although a number of test runs demonstrated that the car was still capable of being operated. This was shown more fully during the summer of 1990 when No 331 was used on the tramway constructed to serve the garden festival held in Gateshead that year. The tram was identified as a suitable candidate for use – it had a large capacity and had had a strong north-eastern connection – and, with sponsorship from British Steel (that resulted in a non-prototypical blue livery), the vehicle was restored to a fully operational condition and initially tested at Crich in 1989. Following its summer on Tyneside, No 331 was returned to Crich and restored to its MET livery. It has been a regular service tram at Crich now for most years since 1991.

Two of the production batch of MET trams also survive. Following their withdrawal in Leeds, Nos 501 (ex-LPTB No 2099) and 526 (ex-LPTB No 2085) were acquired for preservation. The former was to remain in Britain, initially at the Museum of British Transport at Clapham,

Sunderland No 100, looking in a fairly poor condition, seen at Crich on 20 May 1962, shortly after the tram arrived in Derbyshire. Facilities at the museum were limited and a number of trams were stored in the open for a period whilst depot accommodation was constructed.
(Les Collings/Online Transport Archive)

In the early years of tramway preservation, storage was a major problem and a number of tramcars that had been secured were ultimately to be lost, largely due to vandalism. Fortunately, there was the occasional general manager sympathetic to the preservation movement; one of the most notable was Chaceley T. Humpidge at Bradford. Apart from his work in reviving the city's trolleybus system, he also provided facilities for the restoration of Bradford No 104 and permitted the storage of ex-Sunderland No 100 in Thornbury Works. The standard gauge tram – standing, slightly incongruously, on Bradford's 4ft 0in track – was recorded here on 31 October 1959. It was finally to arrive at Crich in 1961. (John Meredith/Online Transport Archive)

whilst the latter was to be exported to the USA and a new home at the Seashore Trolley Museum at Kennebunkport in Maine. No 501 originally arrived at Clapham still in its Leeds livery but was subsequently restored as MET No 355, in 1960. The Clapham Museum, which opened in 1963, was the tram's home until the museum closed in 1973. From 1973 until 1977, it formed part of the London Transport collection at Syon House. With the transfer of the LTM to Covent Garden, a museum that opened in 1980, No 355 was displayed at the new site. Today, No 355 is stored at the LTM's Acton store.

Shipped across the Atlantic in 1960, Leeds No 526 was initially operated by the Seashore Trolley Museum; it has, however, languished in store – albeit

During the summer of 1990, MET No 331 made a return to the north-east of England when it was to be one of the trams employed at that year's Garden Festival at Gateshead. The car, returned as Sunderland No 100, was sponsored by British Steel and was painted in an inauthentic blue and white livery. The tram is seen here at the festival alongside Newcastle No 102, another tram that returned to its home territory for the festival, on 212 May 1990. (R.L. Wilson/Online Transport Archive)

MET No 331 recorded at Wakebridge, at the National Tramway Museum, on 5 July 1997. (Fred Andrews/LRTA (London Area) Collection/Online Transport Archive)

PRESERVATION • 141

A forlorn sight on the Middleton Railway as two ex-Leeds trams stand in derelict condition following vandalism. On the left is 'Horsfield' car No 160 whilst on the right is 'Feltham' No 517; the latter was the only ex-LUT 'Feltham' to be preserved but, unfortunately, it and the majority of the trams stored on the Middleton Railway were eventually to be scrapped. (Harry Luff/Online Transport Archive)

under cover – for a number of years and its condition has deteriorated significantly over the period. The museum is aware of No 526's historical importance and has commented, in response to enquiries about the future of the tram, that it would be willing to transfer the vehicle to another museum provided that this alternative museum has in place a coherent and funded plan for the tram's restoration. It is estimated that transportation and restoration would cost almost £¾ million and so it's unlikely that any UK museum would be in a position to repatriate the tram. Although it doesn't appear at present that No 526 is planned for imminent restoration at Seashore either, the fact that it is under cover is a protection and should it be restored, Seashore has a reputation for the superb quality of this type of work.

A third 'Feltham' – one of the ex-LUT cars No 517 (which had been renumbered from 554 in March 1959 and was ex-LPTB No 2138) – was also secured for preservation. It was one of four trams purchased by the Leeds University Railway Society – the others being 'Horsfield' No 160 and two works cars (overhead car No 1 and ex-Hull No 6). The society initially hoped to be able to rent space under the railway viaduct at Swinegate from British Railways; this, however, did not materialise and, after a period of storage in the open at Swinegate, the quartet was transferred – along with Nos 202 and 601 – to the Middleton Railway. Vandalism at this exposed location, however, resulted in the trams stored there suffering serious damage and most – including the 'Feltham' – were subsequently scrapped.

APPENDIX

The MET 'Felthams'

MET No	LPTB No	Withdrawn	To Leeds	Leeds No	To service	Withdrawn	Scrapped
319	2066	9/50	9/50	506	11/50	5/59	1/60
321	2067	4/49	–	–	–	–	12/49
322	2068	1/51	2/51	539	5/51	11/59	2/60
323	2069	9/50	9/50	505	10/50	8/57	10/57
324	2070	9/50	9/50	507****	11/50	7/53	8/55
325	2071	9/50	1/51	530**	3/51	8/57	10/57
326	2072	9/50	11/50	521	9/51	3/59	7/59
327	2073	9/50	9/50	508	1/51	3/56	8/57
328	2074	9/50	10/50	510	11/50	3/59	7/59
329	2075	9/50	12/50	527	3/51	8/57	10/57
330	2167	4/49	–	–	–	1949	12/49
331	2168	8/36*	–	–	–	–**	–
332	2076	9/50	11/50	524	2/51	10/58	4/59
333	2077	8/50	8/50	503	10/50	4/57	8/57
334	2078	9/50	10/50	509	12/50	12/58	7/59
335	2079	4/51	4/51	550	8/51	9/57	10/57
336	2080	9/50	10/50	516****	1/51	3/57	9/57
337	2081	9/50	11/50	520	1/51	11/59	2/60
338	2082	8/50	9/50	504	10/50	10/59	2/60
339	2083	9/50	12/50	525	3/51	11/59	12/59
340	2084	9/50	7/50	519	2/51	3/59	7/59
341	2085	9/50	12/50	526	3/51	11/59**	–
342	2086	9/50	1/51	528	3/51	7/57	9/57
343	2087	9/50	11/50	518	2/51	1/59	7/59
344	2088	9/50	10/50	512	1/51	11/59	2/60
345	2089	1/51	2/51	537	6/51	5/57	8/57
346	2090	1/51	3/51	544	7/51	6/56	9/57
347	2091	3/49	–	–	–	–	12/49
348	2092	1/51	1/51	533****	4/51	5/57	8/57
349	2093	9/50	10/50	515	1/51	4/59	2/60
350	2094	1/51	2/51	538	5/51	11/59	1/60
351	2095	1/51	3/51	543	6/51	4/57	8/57
352	2096	9/50	11/50	523	9/51	11/59	2/60

MET No	LPTB No	Withdrawn	To Leeds	Leeds No	To service	Withdrawn	Scrapped
353	2097	8/50	8/50	502	10/50	3/59	7/59
354	2098	1/51	3/51	542	6/51	11/59	1/60
355	2099	9/49	10/49	501	12/49	11/59**	–
356	2100	9/50	10/50	513	12/50	12/57	4/59
357	2101	1/51	3/51	546	7/51	5/59	2/60
358	2102	1/51	2/51	534	4/51	6/59	2/60
359	2103	1/51	4/51	548	8/51	3/57	8/57
360	2104	1/51	1/51	532	4/51	11/59	2/60
361	2105	9/50	10/50	511	12/50	8/57	10/57
362	2106	1/51	1/51	531	4/51	11/59	2/60
363	2107	1/51	3/51	541	7/51	10/56	9/57
364	2108	9/50	11/50	522	2/51	2/58	5/59
365	2109	8/44	–	–	–	–	8/44
366	2110	1/51	2/51	536	6/51	12/58	7/59
367	2111	1/51	3/5	545****	7/51	9/57	10/57
368	2112	1/51	4/51	547	7/51	9/57	10/57
369	2113	10/40	–	–	–	–	10/40
370	2114	1/51	2/51	540****	6/51	9/57	10/57
371	2115	9/50	10/50	514	1/51	11/59	2/60
372	2116	9/50	1/51	529	4/51	11/59	2/60
373	2117	1/51	4/51	549	8/51	3/59	7/59
374	2118	9/50	10/50	517	1/51	1/59	5/59
375	2119	1/51	2/51	535	5/51	3/59	7/59

Notes:
   * Sold to Sunderland (No 100)
  ** Preserved cars; No 331 at the National Tramway Museum, No 341 at the Seashore Trolley Museum in the USA and No 355 by the London Transport Museum. No 341 had originally been withdrawn by Leeds Corporation in April 1959 but was restored to service after being retyred.
 *** MVOK9B controller fitted 11/55; it reverted to original MVOK33B controllers in November 1956

   The following cars were renumbered in Leeds
     505 to 520 August 1957
     511 to 519 August 1957
     517 to 554 February 1959
     520 to 505 August 1957
     524 to 565 November 1958
     527 to 528 July 1957 and to 539 August 1957
     528 to 527 July 1957
     539 to 528 August 1957

**** Not fitted with one-piece windscreen between 1955 and 1957

The LUT 'Felthams'

LUT No	LPTB No	Withdrawn	To Leeds	Leeds No	To service	Withdrawn	Scrapped
351	2120	4/51	5/51	557**	12/51	1/59	4/59
352	2121	4/51	5/51	558**	12/51	9/57	10/57
353	2122	1946	–	–	–	–	5/47
354	2123	4/51	6/51	564**	3/55	3/59	7/59
355	2124	4/51	8/51	573**	4/56	2/59	8/59
356	2125	4/51	5/51	561**	4/52	3/59	7/59
357	2126	4/51	6/51	565**	2/55	3/59	7/59
358	2127	4/51	7/61	568**	3/56	3/59	8/59
359	2128	4/51	7/51	(572)***	–	–	11/56
360	2129	4/51	8/51	574**	7/56	3/59	7/59
361	2130	c1948	–	–	–	–	12/49
362	2131	4/51	4/51	555**	11/51	3/56	12/56
363	2132	4/51	7/51	569**	7/55	3/59	8/59
364	2133	4/51	9/51	582**	7/56	3/59	8/59
365	2134	4/51	7/51	566**	3/55	10/57	4/59
366	2135	4/51	9/51	(584)***	–	–	11/56
367	2136	4/51	7/51	567**	4/55	10/57	4/59
368	2137	4/51	5/51	559**	1/52	9/57	11/57
369	2138	4/51	4/51	554**	11/51	5/59*	4/68
370	2139	2/51	3/51	551**/***	10/51	8/56	9/57
371	2140	4/51	6/51	563**	2/55	10/57	4/59
372	2141	4/51	7/51	570**	2/55	9/57	10/57
373	2142	4/51	8/51	(578)***	–	–	9/56
374	2143	4/51	8/51	581**	1/52	1/58	4/59
375	2144	10/50	–	–	–	–	5/51
376	2145	4/51	8/51	(577)***	–	–	8/56
377	2146	4/51	8/51	579**	3/52	3/56	12/56
378	2147	4/51	9/51	587**	6/55	1/59	5/59
379	2148	4/51	5/51	560**	1/52	2/57	9/57
380	2149	4/51	8/51	580**	2/55	9/56	7/57
381	2150	4/51	4/51	553**	11/51	9/57	11/57
382	2151	4/51	8/51	576	–	–	7/56
383	2152	4/51	4/51	556**	12/51	3/59	7/59
384	2153	4/51	9/51	588**	2/52	10/57	4/59
385	2154	4/51	10/51	589**	3/55	3/59	7/59
386	2155	4/51	7/51	(571)***	–	–	11/56
387	2156	4/51	8/51	(575)***	–	–	11/56

LUT No	LPTB No	Withdrawn	To Leeds	Leeds No	To service	Withdrawn	Scrapped
388	2157	4/51	9/51	586**	2/52	9/57	10/57
389	2158	4/51	10/51	590**	5/52	8/57	10/57
390	2159	4/51	9/51	585**	6/56	2/59	7/59
391	2160	4/51	9/51	583**	5/52	3/57	9/57
392	2161	4/51	6/51	562**/***	12/51	8/56	10/57
393	2162	10/50	–	–	–	–	5/51
394	2163	c1948	–	–	–	–	12/49
395	2164	10/50	4/51	552**	11/51	7/56	12/56
396	2165	c1948	–	–	–	–	12/49

Notes:
* Initially preserved and based on the Middleton Railway but body scrapped following serious damage caused by vandalism in April 1968. The bogies were sold to the Tramcar Sponsorship Organisation in 1970 and used in the rebuilding of 'E/1' No 1622, which is now based at the National Tramway Museum.
** Cars fitted with MVOK9B controllers during 1955 and 1956

   The following cars were renumbered
   554 to 517 in February 1959
   557 to 564 in February 1959
   561 to 587 in February 1959
   564 to 557 in February 1959
   565 to 524 in November 1958
   587 to 561 in February 1959

*** Not fitted with one-piece windscreen between 1955 and 1957

BIBLIOGRAPHY

HARLEY, Robert J., *London Tramway Twilight 1949-1952*, Capital Transport; 2000
HARVIE, K.G., *SE London Tramways 1899-1949*, Author; undated
LRTL/LRTA *Modern Tramway*
LRTL/LRTA, *Tramway Review*
OAKLEY, E.R. and HOLLAND, C.E., *London Transport Tramways 1933-1952*, London Transport History Group; 1998
PROUDLOCK, Noel, *Leeds: A History of its Tramways*, published by the author; 1991
REED, John, *London Tramways*, Capital Transport; 1997
SMEETON, C.S., *The London United Tramways: Volume 2 – 1913-1933*, LRTA/TLRS; 2000
SMEETON, C.S., *The Metropolitan Electric Tramways: Volume 2 – 1921-1933*, LRTA/TLRS; 1986
SOPER, J., *Leeds Transport: Volume 3 – 1932-1953*, Leeds Transport Historical Society; 2003
SOPER, J., *Leeds Transport: Volume 4 – 1953-1974*, Leeds Transport Historical Society; 2007
STADDON, S.A., *The Tramways of Sunderland*, Advertiser Press; 1964
WALLER, Michael H. and WALLER, Peter, *British & Irish Tramways Systems since 1945*, Ian Allan Ltd; 1992
WALLER, Peter, *The Classic Trams*, Ian Allan Ltd; 1993
WILLOUGHBY, D.W. and OAKLEY, E.R., *London Transport Tramways Handbook*, published by the authors; 1972
YOUNG, Andrew D., *One Hundred Years of Leeds Tramways*, Turntable Enterprises; 1970